1-11-04

For Walt &
Alice

 W9-BZV-632

Barbara Taylor Bradford's
Living Romantically Every Day

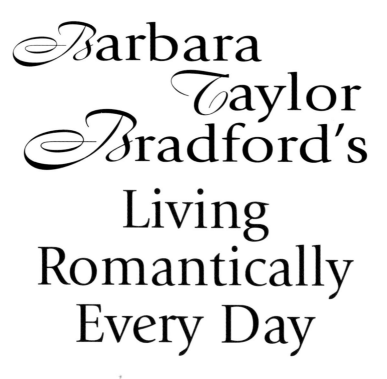

Barbara Taylor Bradford's
Living Romantically Every Day

Barbara Taylor Bradford

Produced by The Philip Lief Group, Inc.

**Andrews McMeel
Publishing**

Kansas City

Barbara Taylor Bradford's Living Romantically Every Day

copyright © 2002 by Barbara Taylor Bradford and The Philip Lief Group, Inc.

All rights reserved. Printed in Singapore.

No part of this book may be used or reproduced in any manner whatsoever
without written permission except in the case of reprints in the context of reviews.
For information, write Andrews McMeel Publishing, an Andrews McMeel Universal
company, 4520 Main Street, Kansas City, Missouri 64111.

Produced by The Philip Lief Group, Inc., 130 Wall Street, Princeton, New Jersey 08540

02 03 04 05 06 TWP 10 9 8 7 6 5 4 3 2 1

Library of Congress Cataloging-in-Publication Data

Bradford, Barbara Taylor, 1933-

    Barbara Taylor Bradford's living romantically every day / Barbara Taylor Bradford

       p. cm

    ISBN 0-7407-2684-6

     1. Man-woman relationships. 2. Love. I. Title: Living romantically every day. II. Title.

HQ801 .B84 2002

306.7—dc21   2002018677

Attention: Schools and Businesses

Andrews McMeel books are available at quantity discounts with bulk
purchase for educational, business, or sales promotional use.
For information, please write to: Special Sales Department,
Andrews McMeel Publishing, 4520 Main Street, Kansas City, Missouri 64111.

For Bob, truly a man for all seasons,
with all my love

Other Books by Barbara Taylor Bradford

A Woman of Substance

Voice of the Heart

Hold the Dream

Act of Will

To Be the Best

The Women in His Life

Remember

Angel

Everything to Gain

Dangerous to Know

Love in Another Town

Her Own Rules

A Secret Affair

Power of a Woman

A Sudden Change of Heart

Where You Belong

The Triumph of Katie Byrne

Three Weeks in Paris

Introduction

Some women insist that men are not romantic. They claim that any romance there is in a relationship springs from the woman, and that it's usually her responsibility to create a sense of romance.

This might well be true, and yet I don't really believe that *all* men are unromantic. Nor do I think it's wise to make generalizations. There's always going to be a maverick in the herd! Then again, I know a number of *women* who are not in the least bit romantic themselves, and, of course, they have their male counterparts who are of similar disposition.

At the opposite side of the spectrum, I have other girlfriends who are the most romantic creatures on earth; also, I am acquainted with several men who are equally as romantic as their spouses—my girlfriends.

Very simply, some people are lucky enough to have a huge dash of romance in their basic natures, while others do not. It's all a question of what you were born with, I suppose.

I myself have been a romantic...for as long as I can remember. Although this comes naturally to me, I'm also aware that my romantic nature was well nurtured when I was growing up in the north of England, however unintentionally.

When I was a young girl living in Yorkshire I was constantly daydreaming... and dipping into books of poetry. Or I was composing poetry of my own, much of it extremely romantic, I recall.

And when I wasn't writing romantic stanzas and dramatic short stories with dying heroines, I had my head in one of the English classics, perhaps a book by one of the Brontë sisters, or Charles Dickens, or the plays of the incomparable William Shakespeare. Each of these great geniuses of English literature wrote about love and romance in the most unique, imaginative and skillful ways.

*M*y mother force-fed all of these marvelous books to me, although I must admit that I never felt as though I was being force-fed anything. I enjoyed every moment of our reading sessions, and everything else we did together.

My mother made me what I am, and I'm quite sure that along the way she filled my head with all kinds of romantic ideas. And ideals. She took me on trips to the city, where we went to the theater, the ballet, the opera, musical comedies, and dramatic plays. And whenever there was a Shakespeare festival we were seated in the front row. And so I learned a great deal about romance...because this exposure fed and enlarged all those inherent notions within me. So did the movies she permitted me to see with her, when she went to the local cinema once a week.

How I loved to sit in the darkened cinema, staring at that magical screen filled with the most glamorous of images. And it was here that I learned about other aspects of love and romance in all its many guises.

My mother loved art and antiques. A big treat for her was to visit some of the impressive stately homes in Yorkshire. I was thrilled whenever she asked me to go along with her.

I remember gazing in awe at extraordinary portraits of aristocrats by such great eighteenth-century portraitists as Sir Thomas Gainsborough and Sir Joshua Reynolds. In these magnificently–built and finely–decorated houses I saw exquisite porcelains, tapestries, and furniture. And the houses themselves evoked images of bygone times when gallant knights abounded and chivalrous deeds flourished on a daily basis, and were actually just a part of the norm.

As many people know from my novels, history has always been one of my favorite subjects, and little bits of history are often woven into my stories. And over the years I have learned a great deal more about romance from historical figures and events that happened in the past. I have read about the royal courts of France at the time of Eleanor of Aquitane, when poets and troubadours wrote of pure, courtly love, and sang of it. And then there were those unique queens who quite naturally were involved in romance, romantic doings, and love in its infinite glories. The greatest of them all, as a monarch and a woman, was Elizabeth I of England, that amazing Tudor queen who often lost her heart to a man but always kept her head—and therefore her throne.

Then there was her cousin, the impossibly romantic and foolish Mary Queen of Scots, who was forever led by her heart and lost her head because of it. And Catherine the Great of Russia, also smart enough to temper her emotions, even though she was dashing and adventurous when it came to love. She, too, died peacefully in her bed, like Elizabeth Tudor.

The knowledge I've acquired has fueled my imagination, and I think that is probably why I became an unrepentant romantic at an early age.

I am very fortunate in that I'm married to a man who is as romantic as I am. During the years we've been together he has planned special dinners in romantic spots around the world, just for the two of us... brought home flowers or a gift when I've least expected it...a bottle of perfume, a book of poems, or some other book he thought I would enjoy... whatever it was it was special, because Bob had thought of me, and of pleasing me.

Some gifts have been more elaborate. He once came back from making a movie in Paris, bringing with him my favorite Kelly bag from Hermès. On another occasion, when he was filming a mini-series in London, he FedExed a cream silk raincoat he had seen in the window of a boutique because he thought the color was perfect for a blonde. His blonde.

But to be truthful, it's the notes, cards, and letters that he has sent me over the past forty years that mean so much, and which I treasure the most. His words are extraordinarily meaningful, especially to someone so conscious of words like me.

Whilst I know how lucky I am to have a loving and romantic husband such as Bob, some of my girlfriends are lucky too. One close friend was truly surprised by her husband recently, during the week of her birthday. Unbeknownst to her, he had been to a jewelry auction and had successfully bid on a set of matching pearl pieces: earrings, a flower pin, and a bracelet. On the night before her birthday she found the pearl pin under her pillow, the next night the earrings, and on the third night of the birthday week the bracelet was tucked into the same spot. Not only was she bowled over by the beautiful gifts but touched and thrilled by his romantic way of giving them to her.

Another friend was proposed to by her boyfriend in a house she had always dreamed of owning. Unexpectedly, it had come on the market, and although neither of them could afford to buy it, her boyfriend had arranged with the real estate broker to rent it for one night. In the empty dining room he set up a small table and chairs, covered the table with a white cloth, added a bowl of white roses and silver candlesticks. After making a fire in the hearth, he then went to collect his lady love, my friend. As he drove her off to dinner he explained that they were going to have a picnic instead. Which they did. In her dream house.

In the candlelight, with the fire blazing in the background, he poured Champagne, served caviar and smoked salmon, and promised to buy her a house just like this. One day. Then he produced a sapphire engagement ring and asked her to marry him. Of course she said yes.

So you see there *are* men who are just as romantic as women, given half the chance. My mother always remarked that it was a woman who made a relationship work, and for years I really believed that. But eventually I came to understand that this is not always the case. In my opinion, it takes two people.

Although falling in love might just happen, in the flick of an eye, so to speak, having a loving relationship that grows, flourishes, and endures requires quite a lot of nurturing, tender loving care, if you will. Plus skill and knowledge as well. And just the right amount of romance is part of that nurturing. It might even take a little work, but being romantic with someone you love is *fun* work. If one half of the couple has a deficit in this area, or isn't naturally romantic, it's important that the other partner takes the initiative, fosters romance, and makes it an integral part of the relationship. After all, who doesn't want to be showered with love and affection part of the time. It's what makes the world go round, I think.

In many ways I was fortunate in that I learned about romance early, through books and plays, poetry, music, and art. Thanks to my mother. And all of these things helped me to truly develop the inherent tendency in my nature to be a romantic.

And so perhaps some of my thoughts and ideas and guidelines here will help you to foster your natural instincts for romance. Or help you to learn about it...and maybe you and your partner will both become unrepentant romantics like me and Bob.

Barbara Taylor Bradford

Chapter 1

LIVING
for
Romance

Romance isn't really about Champagne and flowers—though those are wonderful elements. At its core, romance is about how we choose to live our lives. It's about respecting certain principles and being open to the wonders of the world around us. It involves taking chances. Ultimately, it helps us live life to its fullest. Let romance into your life every day…starting now.

what it MEANS
to be *Romantic*

I know that we each have our own personal definition of what it means to be romantic, but there are some common elements. Say the word "romance" and you might conjure up images of being swept off your feet, of dramatic moments, and grand gestures. And while I won't say that these fantasies aren't in themselves romantic, I will say that they merely scratch the surface of what it means to be romantic.

❖ Being romantic is actually a form of communication—your words and actions translate into an expression of love for your partner. In its strictest sense, romance can be defined as an ardent attachment between two people. But to my mind, romance is in the bonds that create, strengthen, and maintain that attachment.

❖ Being romantic means truly understanding your partner. It means always offering your whole-hearted support.

❖ Being romantic means treating each and every day as a wonderful possibility. Life is not a dress rehearsal. As far as we know, we only get one chance to come through this world, and it is up to us to make the most of it.

❖ Being romantic is a way to savor every moment and ultimately to enjoy this unique journey we're taking.

WHY BE *Romantic* every day?

If you think that being romantic requires you to whisk your lover away to Venice or to write prolific love sonnets, you'll dismiss the thought that you can live romantically every day. Because of the pressures already on us from work, children, social commitments, and other responsibilities, we often feel that we simply can't squeeze another thing into our days. I know this firsthand: When I am under deadline working on a book, it's very difficult to break away from that. Being romantic becomes a chore and gets pushed aside. But I believe that being romantic every day is not a luxury; it is the very essence of how you conduct your life.

❖ Being romantic means expressing your affection by showing your partner respect, loyalty, generosity, compassion, honesty, and integrity—special qualities I focus on in the "Secrets to Love" section in each chapter. They are woven into the fabric of our daily lives and enhance our relationships with our partners.

❖ Being romantic means truly listening to your partner. You may not have the time to go out for a big night on the town, but you always have time to open your heart to each other. I call this "tuning in." Communication is at the heart of romance and you will find information about this topic in Chapter 3.

❖ Being romantic means embracing the spirit of spontaneity and adventure. Being open to the possibilities of the world around you is the hallmark of a true romantic.

❖ Being romantic means remembering that you are the heroine of your own life. The female protagonists in my novels are strong, complex women—just like the women I know in real life.

why ROMANCE is *Essential*

*A*n old saying claims that variety is the spice of life, but I personally believe that romance is. A life lived without romance is a cold and empty prospect to me. I feel blessed with good fortune in my life, but the most important part of that has been my husband, Bob. After thirty-eight years of marriage, I think I can say with confidence that romance is essential. These are my reasons why:

❖ Romance makes you feel special. There is nothing as wonderful as knowing that you love and are loved in return.

❖ Romance keeps you young in mind and spirit. Ponce de León never discovered the Fountain of Youth, but if such a thing existed, I think it would simply be love and romance.

romantic california

California, from the rocky northern coastline to the warm beaches in the south, is full of romantic destinations. In Los Angeles, the Hotel Bel-Air has always been one of my favorite places to stay. Tucked away in the elegant community of Bel-Air, the hotel is surrounded by gardens that are some of the loveliest I've ever seen: lush and tropical, with blue-blossomed jacaranda trees, a fifty-foot pink floss tree, a tranquil waterfall, and an arching stone bridge over a lake filled with white swans. Britain's royal family, presidents, and the biggest names in Hollywood have stayed in its ninety-two Mediterranean-style rooms, none of which are alike. Bob and I like the Swan Lake Suite—its patio, garden, and view of the swan pond have a pastoral feeling. We enjoy eating lunch in the fabulous patio restaurant—a great way to enjoy the hotel even if a stay there is out of your price range. At night, the main dining room is elegant yet charming and unpretentious.

I think the reason I love this hotel so much is that it embodies the spirit of California—naturally elegant, verdant, and luxurious but in many ways low-key and relaxed. Other parts of Los Angeles to enjoy as a couple include Santa Monica, with its fine shops, promenade, and the Santa Monica Pier with its famed carousel. The unspoiled beauty of Catalina Island, which lies just twenty-two miles out from the Los Angeles coastline, is hypnotic, from its mountainous terrain to its beaches. The island's only real town, Avalon, is a beach community where palm trees still line the main street. If you visit California, seek out other magnificent and less developed beaches, such as Santa Barbara's East Beach, Big Sur's Sand Dollar Beach, and Torrey Pines, near San Diego.

Equally beautiful is northern California, where the vineyards of Napa Valley and Sonoma produce some of the best wines in the world. With plenty of vineyards to tour (don't miss the gondola ride up to Sterling Vineyards), many of which offer wine tastings; outstanding restaurants, such as French Laundry, Auberge du Soleil (also a gorgeous inn), Tra Vigne, and Mustard's Grill; and lovely inns and B&Bs, this area is a great romantic and honeymoon destination.

San Francisco has been called the most European of American cities (stay in one of the Victorian B&Bs), with its historic cable cars, unique pier (home to sea lions), the spectacular Golden Gate Bridge, famed shopping in Union Square, and fine dining—try the French-California cuisine of Charles Nob Hill, named San Francisco's most romantic restaurant by *Bon Appetit* magazine. Here are some ways to bring the golden glow of California into your home:

❱ Bring fine California wine to your table. Some vintners to look for are Kendall Jackson, Rutherford Hill, Geyser Peak, and Chalk Hill. To sample wines from the lesser-known "boutique" vintners, consider joining a wine club; members of the California Wine Club (www.cawineclub.com) receive two bottles a month (one white, one red) and a newsletter on the featured wineries.

❱ Fresh produce is the hallmark of California cuisine, and farmers' markets are the most popular way to shop for delectable fruit and vegetables. Look for a farmers' market near your home and check out the offerings.

❱ The *Queen Mary*, once a renowned luxury ocean liner now moored at Long Beach, hosts a famous Sunday Champagne brunch. Prepare your own Champagne brunch and play classical music. Brunch on the *Queen Mary* features a harpist; try the recordings of world-famous harpist Yolanda Kondonassis.

❤ Romance makes us realize there are many sides to our personalities. Many people define themselves by the role they play, such as wife or mother, or by the job they do. But being romantic means you are someone's lover; you are the person who makes his or her heart sing. Never forget that.

❤ Romance brings out our best selves. To truly love another person requires maturity and strength, generosity and compassion. By lifting us beyond our own concerns, it enables us to think of another person before we think of ourselves.

❤ Romance makes the ups and downs easier to bear. It doesn't promise to make our paths easy, but it certainly guarantees a wonderful journey!

❤ Romance helps us keep our lives in perspective. When you make time for romance, you're saying that you choose love. Jobs, material possessions; even friends, may come and go, but romance can be there for you always. It's a constant—and it's what matters most.

CREATING a *Relationship* mission statement

*C*orporate partnerships and new businesses don't move forward without a mission statement; I think it's a good idea for personal partnerships as well. Many people fall in love without really knowing their partner; they may know all sorts of facts about him, but they haven't yet explored what his deeply held and fervently felt values and beliefs are. A true, lasting partnership demands a "merger" of goals, dreams, and principles. Here are some ways to develop your own relationship mission statement:

❖ Plan a quiet evening with some of your favorite nibbles. Before the "meeting," sit down and list your own personal life goals, and ask your partner to do the same. Then get together to compare lists. You might find that they're quite similar—or they may be wildly divergent. Talk about what's on your lists and make clear what the priorities are.

❖ Next, work to create a list together. On your own personal list, you might have included career goals for yourself or a goal such as "learn a second language." On your "partnership list," write down the things you want to achieve together. This could include anything from having children (how many and timing are also important considerations) or not having children to buying a home (what style, location) to traveling to a particular far-flung part of the globe. Think carefully also about issues such as religion and community involvement. Whatever you agree on is valid and goes into your mission statement.

❧ Have each of you write a specific statement about what qualities in a spouse or partner are most important to you. I believe that your spouse should be your friend and lover, your true confidante, the person closest to you in the world, and the person who helps you realize your dreams and live your life well. You might think about the qualities I mentioned earlier, such as respect, loyalty, generosity, compassion, honesty, and integrity—that above all.

❧ While the relationship with your partner is at the core of your world, you also need to determine which other people fit into your partnership. Other relationships are important and enrich different parts of your life together: You may list your children's godparents, the two or three couples you most enjoy spending time with, or others with whom you have a relationship. Be specific in stating how they fit into your life.

❧ Your relationship mission statement should also focus on what you are going to do to further your partnership. In this way, the relationship becomes more than the sum of two individuals. Decisions need to be made on the basis of what's necessary for the relationship to survive—and thrive. While of course we each have our own needs to be met, the needs of the partnership should be considered first. This is a helpful approach if you're faced with a big decision, such as moving across the country to accept a job. You might plan to set aside a half hour each week to fill each other in on concerns and issues or to make plans for the upcoming month, reserving this time to talk only about things that directly impact your relationship.

❧ Reevaluate your mission statement at regular intervals. It could be every three months or every year; you might choose your anniversary, for example. As your relationship continues to grow, your mission statement will need tuning.

$\mathcal{R}omance$ and the FIVE SENSES

We are endowed with five wonderful gifts with which we experience the world around us: sight, sound, touch, taste, and smell. A true romantic has a sensual appreciation of what the world has to offer. Being a novelist has only reinforced my respect for the magic of the senses, because I know how essential they are to setting a scene and capturing atmosphere, nuance, and drama—whether in fiction or in real life. Try these ideas to celebrate your senses:

❧ Breaking our routines, even just a little bit, heightens our sensual awareness. If you always take the same route to work or to the grocery store, you won't experience the different aspects of your environment with the heightened sense of the new. Make a point of going off your beaten path and open your eyes.

❧ Stop and smell the roses—and I mean this literally. Keeping your eye on your watch prevents you from gaining inspiration from the natural wonders that surround you. Slow down a little bit to focus more fully on what shade of blue the sky is today. Create a visual imprint in your mind to carry with you through the day.

❧ Let your tactile sense guide you. Does what you're wearing feel good against your skin? If not, no matter how pretty it looks on, it's not a keeper. What's more romantic than wearing your partner's well-worn flannel shirt? It's a hug you carry with you all day. Hold your partner's hand and concentrate on the warmth and the texture of his skin.

❧ Expand your taste horizons. Try new cuisines, either in a restaurant or in your own kitchen, for a sensual experience. Or, try a new food or exotic fruit you've never tried before.

❧ Listening to your partner's voice is a romantic experience in and of itself, though it's hard to focus on his timbre and pitch when you're having a conversation. Ask him to read to you, close your eyes, and just focus on his voice. Later, do the same for him. Find a new piece of music you love and share it with your partner.

The Incurable Romantic

scents of love: *perfume*

Of all of our senses, smell is the most evocative. We take in the smells around us consciously and unconsciously, and I know only too well that years later they still stir up memories with great clarity. I have a friend who tells me that every time she smells Pacquin hand cream, the scent takes her right back to when she was a child and loved to watch her mother getting ready to go out: the red lipstick, the curlers, the Jackie Kennedy-style dresses. And I myself find the decades falling away when I smell Yardley's English Lavender water, which my mother always used, and I am carried back to my childhood.

❧ The Egyptians incorporated perfume into their religious rituals. To me, wearing perfume is a daily pleasure, and it can be for you, too. I have several favorite perfumes: Rouge by Hermès, Diorella by Christian Dior, Joy by Jean Patou, First by Van Cleef & Arpels, and Fracas by Robert Piguet. Whenever I use another favorite, Ma Griffe by Carven, I am suddenly swept back to the years I lived in Paris as a journalist in my twenties.

❧ The distilleries in Grasse, the perfume capital of France, in Provence, date back to the sixteenth century. The region is rich in jasmine, rose, orange, and lavender. The perfumer Jean Patou maintains fields of jasmine and May rose here, and its jasmine, a particularly fragile flower, is picked only by hand and at dawn. It takes 10,600 jasmine flowers to make a single ounce of Joy perfume.

❧ Renowned perfume houses such as Guerlain, founded in 1828, established Paris as the first commercial center of the perfume trade. One of my own favorite Guerlain fragrances is Jicky.

❧ Perfume makers partnered with crystal manufacturers such as Baccarat and Lalique to produce stunning perfume bottles. I collect Baccarat and Lalique bottles as well as cut-crystal English ones—all antiqués. Decorative bottles add a romantic touch to the bedroom or bathroom.

❧ There are several scent families. Florals, my personal favorite, include gardenia, lily of the valley, and tuberose. Fruity scents capture elements of passionfruit, melon, or neroli. Citrus has notes of mandarin, grapefruit, or bergamot. Green fragrances feature juniper, lavender, or rosemary. Oriental scents use musk, vanilla, and amber. Spicy perfumes contain cinnamon, cardamom, and cloves.

❧ Choose your scent carefully. The best way to test a perfume is to wear it for a little while, so spritz some on at the perfume counter and see if you like the scent as much several hours later. The chemistry of each individual's skin affects the scent of a perfume.

❧ Layering fragrance is a wonderful way to wrap yourself in scent. If you love a certain fragrance, see if it is available in a soap, a bath foam, or moisturizer. Using two or three same-scented products helps the scent last longer. Keep an eau de toilette bottle in your purse for a "refresher" during the day.

SECRETS to love: *Honesty*

If you look at all of the elements that combine to make love possible, one of the essentials is honesty. It is the foundation upon which love is built. Without honesty, there is no trust or respect. Acceptance is one of the keys to love, but you cannot reach it across a bridge of untruths. And you cannot be loyal to a person who hides behind a mask of deception.

A *strict definition of honesty* would tell us that it includes truthfulness. That's right, but there's more than that to honesty. It is also based on sincerity and integrity. Honesty takes courage, too, because it demands that we reveal our unvarnished selves. But the rewards honesty offers are great, since showing our true colors is the only way to open ourselves up to love. Here are some ways to express honesty with the one you love:

❧ *Be honest with your partner about issues big and small.* I think we already know that it's wrong to lie about important issues in your life and relationship, but I think it's a sad mistake to lie about small matters, too. When our partner expresses an interest or an opinion about something, it is easy to respond reflexively by saying, "Yes, I think that, too." If you disagree, ask him why he feels the way he does and discuss your differences of opinion. Agreeing to disagree is healthy. There's nothing romantic about a person who doesn't think for herself.

❧ *Be honest, but don't use the truth as a weapon.* We are all familiar with the expression: "The truth hurts." It doesn't have to. Using the "honesty" approach to say hurtful words to your partner is simply cruel. Temper your honesty with respect, humility, and acceptance (see pages 55, 133, and 166).

❧ *Be honest about your hopes and dreams.* There's also nothing romantic about ignoring your own plans and living someone else's. Share what's in your heart and mind with your partner—and encourage him to be equally honest with you.

❧ *Be honest with yourself.* Do you believe you're living the life that makes you happy, or do you think that you need to change things? Try to be as objective as possible. Let the small stuff go, but give bigger issues the attention they deserve. When you're honest with yourself, you foster honesty in your relationship.

Tasting the Stars:
CHAMPAGNE

I don't think anything spells out romance and celebration as instantly as Champagne. It's the perfect romantic drink: Light and effervescent, it pairs up beautifully with just about anything, though it goes especially well with caviar. Genuine Champagne comes only from the Champagne region of France. My personal favorites are Veuve Clicquot and Dom Perignon, which is named for the seventeenth-century monk who discovered Champagne. According to legend, he ran to his fellow friars and said, "Brothers, I am tasting the stars!" My great hero, Sir Winston Churchill, favored Pol Roger Champagne. In our bar at home, we have a wonderful lithograph of Sir Winston looking down on some of his favorites, including Pol Roger, cognacs, and his cigars. It was painted by his granddaughter, Edwina Sandys, a friend of ours, who gave it to us for our thirty-fifth wedding anniversary. I love this painting.

Champagne is made from either Chardonnay or Pinot Noir grapes. Like your Champagne dry or slightly sweet? Specific names, which you'll find on the label, indicate the actual level of sugar, which ranges from 0.5 to 1.25 percent. In order, from driest to sweetest: natural (sometimes called *brut*

naturel), brut, extra dry (or *sec*), and rose (*rouge*). I learned quite a lot about Champagne and wines when doing research for my novel *Dangerous to Know*. In that book, one of the characters, Jack Locke, owns a vineyard in France, and since I always like to give a sense of authenticity, I read a lot about grape growing and the making of wine.

The process of making Champagne starts out like that of most wines; the difference is that eventually yeast and sugar are added, creating carbon dioxide—that's where the bubbles come from. The bottle is turned on a regular basis for months or even years, and then the cork is popped to remove the sediment, and a new cork is put in.

I only serve Champagne in tall glasses, called flutes, rather than bowl glasses. Flutes are traditional for serving Champagne, but more important, their narrow shape keeps the bubbles from dissipating too quickly, and it concentrates the lovely scent of the wine, too. The thinness of the glass is important; look carefully before you buy. I use a special pair of engraved silver flutes that my British publisher gave to me on the twentieth anniversary of the publication of my first novel, *A Woman of Substance*. With the silver flutes came a bottle of Dom Perignon and a tin of Triple 0 caviar. I felt very spoiled, and so did Bob. For more information on caviar and how to serve it, see "Food for Love," page 72.

The Romantic Gourmet

Chapter 2

CREATING
time for
Romance

Seize the day—and the hours and the minutes. Spending time together is essential to living romantically every day. Don't wait for perfect moments. You have the power to create them yourself. I believe that all it takes is a spirit of giving from the heart—and some creative thinking—to find time for romance to thrive. A stolen moment, the gift of time, a thoughtful expression of love, all help to make love grow and set the heart aflutter.

stealing *Time* TOGETHER

I *know one of my greatest challenges is figuring out how to meet my many obligations and manage a very full writing schedule while still having time to spend with my husband, Bob, to enjoy each other's company and nurture romance. Remember your priorities: Enjoying each other's company isn't a frill; it's an essential part of your day. Here are some ways I've found to do this:*

❖ Turn the ringer off the phone at a regular time, such as in the evenings or on weekends, to give yourselves some uninterrupted time together. You can always return calls later—and you won't mind missing the telephone solicitations.

❖ Get up a half hour earlier than usual. Use that time to enjoy a cup of frothy cappuccino together, talk about something on your mind or something important about the day, or just enjoy each other's company in the peace of the morning before the hectic day begins.

❖ Take on some tasks together. It might seem efficient to divvy up the chores separately, but by doing some of the work together, like going through those stacked-up piles of photos to organize them into

an album, you guarantee yourselves an opportunity to share some time—and probably some laughter.

❖ Leave an event just a little bit early. No one will mind your departure, and this will give you at least a few moments to be alone together. There's the added thrill of feeling like you're playing hooky together, too.

❖ Even if you're busy with different projects, work on them while you're close by each other. Your partner's presence in the same room is a boost, even if you have to set conversation aside for now.

❖ Schedule time each week for a "date" just with each other, even if it means giving up something else, like a class at the gym. You might choose to eat breakfast out once a week, rent a movie and put the bills and mail aside for one night, or cook one special meal together once a week to enjoy each other's company and focus on you as a couple. You might just spend an uninterrupted hour talking, catching up, dreaming together—simply indulging in the much-needed luxury of focusing on yourselves. What you do on your "date" might change each week, and the time you commit to might also change, but by each Sunday night, make sure you've set aside a date for the upcoming week.

Gifts from the HEART

*E*verybody loves gifts—especially those that come from the heart. It is most important when giving a gift to think of what your partner really wants and needs and to remember that giving the perfect gift isn't about spending a great deal of money or hunting for the one perfect item; it's about considering your partner's needs and interests and responding to them. Gifts from the heart need not wait for a special day—a gift makes any day special. Some of the best gifts from the heart are free and require only a little creativity. What's essential is that they be wrapped in love. Some suggestions:

❖ Give your partner several sealed "mystery" envelopes. Inside each one you'll have put a coupon for a personal gift, such as a massage or a favorite meal— little indulgences that you know your partner loves. When your partner wants to "order" a gift, he will open one of the envelopes…then it's up to you to deliver.

❖ Create a memory album with photographs of just the two of you, from when you first met up to the present. Make funny

captions and include as much detail as you can remember, such as the name of the great dessert you had at that fabulous restaurant on your vacation or how you got lost but discovered a beautiful scenic spot. You might also include favorite comic strips, tickets from concerts or movies, postcards from places you've traveled to together, and so on. Leave extra pages to fill in your future. They make wonderful "memory trips" later on. I've made several albums for Bob. Two have been "pictorial recordings" of movies he's made of my books, *Voice of the Heart* and *Hold the Dream*, each one with off-camera shots of stars, other cast members, and Bob himself. I also did another album featuring our Bichon Frise, Gemmy, who died in 1992.

❖ Buy your love's favorite dessert when you're on your way home. Enjoy it while you talk after dinner or as a midnight snack (see "The Romantic Gourmet: Midnight Snacks," page 77, for ideas).

❖ Research romantic lore and legends and write them on little pieces of paper. Tape a different one to the bathroom mirror each day for a week. Example: Why do we wear wedding rings on the "ring finger"? The ancient Greeks and Romans believed that a nerve ran from that finger directly to the heart.

❖ Try to do something nice for your partner every day. Making a simple phone call, bringing home dinner, or tucking a secret love note or romantic quote, even a simple "I miss you!" scribbled on a piece of paper, into his jacket pocket does the trick.

❖ Create a picnic in your own backyard under the evening stars (see "Tips for a Perfect Picnic," page 45, for ideas). Turn the backyard into a fantasy. Drape the trees and fences with tiny white lights and decorate the porch. Turn on slow music and dance under the moon.

❖ Pack your love a "custom" lunch with his or her favorite items and write a secret note or romantic quote on a napkin.

❖ When tensions run high, book a special dinner at your favorite restaurant and promise each other not to talk "money" or "the house," or whatever the bone of contention is, for the entire evening.

❖ On a cold morning, go out and warm up your spouse's car before he or she leaves for work.

❖ Write him a love letter—by hand! (See "The Incurable Romantic: Love Letters," page 50, for inspiration.)

the romance of *Nature*

One of the most romantic places you'll ever discover is the great outdoors. The quiet, pure beauty of nature never fails to stir my emotions. Here are some ways to indulge in the magical allure of nature to inspire romance:

❧ Look at nature in a new light by going for a walk together at different times of the day. Instead of strolling at dusk, try going out early in the morning. The quality of the light will change everything you see around you.

❧ Make a date to watch the sunset together. It's nature's greatest painting.

❧ Visit the great outdoors near where you live on a weekend or plan a vacation around a scenic destination. With a little research, you might discover pretty walking trails in some hidden woods, a languid canoe ride or picnic site along the banks of a quiet river, a day excursion to the seaside, or the tranquillity of an outdoor Japanese water garden.

❧ Play outside together. Nature inspires a childlike sense of fun. Build sand castles, romp in leaves, make snow angels.

❧ On a warm summer night, spread a blanket on the lawn or go to a park. Gaze at the beautiful stars. Listen to the symphony of night birds and crickets.

The Incurable Romantic
finding *romantic* restaurants

When you and your love can give yourselves the gift of time to enjoy a night out, make the most of the evening by finding a romantic restaurant.

First, figure out your "wish list." Perhaps you long for a quiet, candlelit meal that allows you to gaze into each other's eyes without interruption. Or maybe you'd prefer to dine in a lively, vibrant room that hums with music and conversation. Think, too, about the sort of cuisine you enjoy: French equals romance in many minds, but Italian or Thai can be just as delightful. Great service is another joy of dining out: Would you like to have a waiter hovering discreetly but attentively or would you prefer a little more privacy and "invisible" service? It's entirely up to you.

One caveat: Don't fall into the trap of thinking that more expensive equals more romantic. Some of the most romantic restaurants I've found in my travels have been small, family-run gems. Here are tips for finding a romantic spot to dine *à deux* in your own area or when you travel:

◗ Leaf through local newspapers, city magazines, restaurant guides, and area guidebooks to see what restaurants are listed as romantic. Around Valentine's Day, most local publications run articles about romantic places to dine out; clip and save. Sometimes looking at a print ad for a restaurant can give you a sense of its ambience.

◗ Contact restaurant critics by letter or phone. Briefly describe what you're looking for and ask for recommendations. Most will be happy to oblige with a short list.

◗ Ask for referrals from friends and acquaintances. Do keep in mind that everyone will not find the same spots romantic, but if you mention your "wish list," for example, a quiet spot that serves Spanish paella or Italian pastries, you should pick up some good ideas.

◗ Check with a hotel concierge, who should have up-to-the-minute information as well as firsthand opinions from hotel guests.

◗ Call the restaurants on your short list so that you're spared any surprises. Tell them that you're planning a romantic dinner, and ask about the noise level, wine list, whether there's live music, or any other concern or requirement you have. If possible, drop by the restaurant for a quick visit. Just stepping in the door lets you soak up a little ambience, and you can glance at the menu. Or you can do an online visit; many restaurants have Web sites and post their menus, sometimes with photographs.

33

overcoming *Obstacles*
to romance

*N*o matter how deep and strong your love is, you and your partner are likely, every now and then, to encounter obstacles in your relationship. Remember, as the old saying goes, the course of true love never runs smooth. You need to address difficulties, large or small, in order to live your life together to its fullest— and most romantic—potential.

Start by identifying what your own obstacles to romance are as a couple. Every couple is different; your roadblocks may change during the different "seasons" of your relationship.

To get a sense of your obstacles, start by imagining what an ideal romantic day with your partner would be like. Where would you be? What would you be doing? When you have your picture clearly in mind, list the things that fall in the way of your ideal. Below are some of what I think are the most common obstacles to

romance, followed by suggestions of how to manage them in order to make more room for romance every day.

work

It's frustrating when work creates obligations such as overtime at the office or take-home work on weekends that devour your precious time. When work overwhelms, add a touch of romance to those days:

❖ Telephone your partner to say that you're thinking about him. Keep it short but sweet: You needn't linger on the phone; just add a ray of sunshine to his day by reminding him he is important to you or that you are still crazy about him after all these years together.

✤ Drop by your love's office with a care package when he or she is working late. It can be simple: A gourmet coffee and a hot meal will be appreciated by anyone trapped in the office. And if you don't have time to drop by in person or it doesn't make logistical sense, order a gourmet meal for delivery.

✤ Communicate about what you're working on. If one of you has a demanding project, let the other know about it and how long you think it will last. This avoids hurt feelings and lets your partner know there's light at the end of the tunnel.

✤ Plan a special day together when the deadline's over to give your partner something to look forward to and to give you something fun to think about and to occupy the time you're missing your partner at work.

stress

Stressors are little demons that cloud our vision of romance and our ability to prioritize our relationship. Next time you or your partner's buttons are being pushed by a situation in the outside world, here are some ways to nurture a sense of calm:

✤ Set aside a few minutes every day for you and your partner to release steam from your day. The person speaking holds the floor; the person listening cannot offer advice or an opinion, unless it's asked for. Be a sounding board.

✤ Touch is a great soother and reminds you that you're well loved and appreciated. Hold hands when you're talking together; give each other a big, long hug.

✤ Discover the healing power of laughter. It's a great tension reliever. For more on the importance of a sense of humor, see "The Gift of Laughter," page 71.

✤ Give a foot massage—no training needed. Work your fingers and thumbs deeply into the sole and arch of the foot—too light a touch tickles. Gently work the toes, then hold and caress the foot.

✤ Create your own at-home aromatherapy treatment, the centuries-old practice of using fragrant oils—sandalwood, rose, lavender, eucalyptus, mint—to induce relaxation. Burn aromatherapy candles or use the oils for massage or the bath.

children

If you have children, no doubt you'd name your cherubs as a key deterrent to making time for romance in your marriage. Here's how to balance your needs with theirs:

❧ All parents need time to themselves to reconnect. Make a commitment to hire a babysitter on a regular basis and let yourselves get away, even if only for a couple of hours. To save money, work out an "exchange" with the parents of one of your child's friends: You watch their child one evening or afternoon a month and they watch yours another time.

❧ You and your partner need to be alone together for a part of each and every day. Put your children to bed at a reasonable hour; now you have time for each other.

❧ Have your child take a Saturday morning art, music, or dance class. Your child benefits from an enriching activity and you and your spouse get a weekly hour of time to steal away to a nearby park or café.

❧ A few times a year, take a day off together while your kids are in school.

❧ When your children are old enough, arrange for them to spend the weekend with grandma or close friends. Stay at home and enjoy your quiet house or plan a getaway, such as a drive to a country inn or B&B.

❧ Plan vacations to destinations that offer supervised children's activities so you and your spouse can steal away for a few hours.

SECRETS to love: *Consideration*

So often when we think about romance we think of how it makes us feel— and is there anything better than feeling loved? Perhaps only one thing: making your partner feel loved. Romance isn't about fulfilling just your own needs; the deepest, most satisfying love comes from putting your partner first. Consideration lies at the heart of this.

Consideration means showing thoughtful concern and regard for your partner's feelings, space, time, and needs. This careful thinking can take the form of small, simple gestures that speak volumes. Showing consideration is an open demonstration of love that you can practice every day. Don't confuse consideration with self-sacrifice:

It's not about giving up what you want to meet your partner's needs. Rather consideration gives you both what you need.

Consideration is solidly grounded in a strong knowledge of your partner. It requires that you really listen and tune in to your partner on a daily basis. You need to know what he cares about, what's important to him, and what's on his mind on any given day. How can you be considerate of your partner? Here are my suggestions:

❖ *Be considerate of your partner's feelings.* If your partner's anxious, don't brush it off by saying, "Oh, honey, don't make this into a big deal." Validate his or her feelings by saying, "I know you're really anxious about tomorrow. Let's get up a half hour early. I'll make your favorite breakfast and we can go over your game plan once more before you go."

❖ *Be considerate of your partner's space.* Don't move or reorganize your partner's personal items, paperwork, or project because you think your way is better. If you think, for example, that the light on his desk is poor, don't make a disparaging remark; surprise him with a desk lamp in a style you think

he'll love. Part of being considerate of your partner's space also means sensing when he needs time alone and giving him that without whining, asking questions, or taking it personally.

❖ *Be considerate of your partner's time.* If your partner is rushed, don't start a big discussion or complain; instead, offer to help lighten the load. Offer to call or hail a cab or brew some coffee to go. Also, if your partner likes to get information in short bites, don't be verbose; explain your point in one or two clear sentences.

❖ *Be considerate of your partner's needs.* If your partner needs a half hour to unwind after work, let him. Or, if your partner really enjoys spending time with his brother, whom you don't care for, use that time to do things on your own or to get together with your own friends. If your partner needs to vent about something—even something you're tired of hearing about, like his difficult father or tiresome boss— always listen with patience and support. You'd want the same in return.

provençal
picnic à deux

This menu was inspired by my novel Remember, *in which the main character, Nicky, stays at her friend Clee's farmhouse in beautiful Provence in the south of France. A picnic is such a wonderful romantic mini-getaway. Much of this menu, which features the classic Salade Niçoise and a choice of two desserts—try one now and save the other for another picnic excursion, can be made ahead of time; see the box "Countdown to Success," page 39. I've also included a Picnic Checklist, page 44, so you don't forget a thing. Here are some ideas to make your picnic especially romantic:*

❖ Along with the essentials, pack a book of romantic poetry. After lunch, ask your partner to lie with his or her head in your lap and read poetry in the mid-afternoon sun.

❖ Bring fresh flowers to your picnic. Pack a wide-bottomed, low vase or a pretty ceramic or glass bowl that won't tip over easily, a plastic quart bottle filled with cold water, and a bunch of flowers you've either purchased or plucked from your garden that morning. Double wrap the stems in damp paper towels and then in foil. Pack scissors with your flatware. At the picnic, pour the water into the vase or bowl, trim the flower stems to the desired length, and create a casual on-site arrangement.

❖ Write your partner a secret note containing a short romantic message or list the three things you love most about him or her. Roll it into a napkin or tuck it under the dessert plate for a sweet surprise that's sure to touch the heart.

❖ Try a sunset picnic—twilight can be a magical time of day…and so pretty. Add votive candles and matches to your checklist, and pack a sweater for each of you or, better yet, a soft, cozy throw to cuddle under as you watch the stars come out.

Menu

Honeydew Ribbons and Cantaloupe with Blueberries

Salade Niçoise

Walnut Tartlets
or
Pears Poached in Red Wine

Honeydew Ribbons and Cantaloupe with Blueberries

Begin your picnic with this fresh fruit mélange—très francais. You might come across a Cavaillon, the famous melon of Provence, at a specialty food store but, if not, a ripe cantaloupe is perfect. I like to use a wide vegetable peeler to create ribbons of honeydew; however, if you prefer, simply cut the honeydew into very long thin slices with a paring knife. You can also skip the melon baller and just cut the cantaloupe into small cubes. Either way, it looks best if you arrange the honeydew on the bottom of the dish and then scatter the cantaloupe on top.

¹/₂ small ripe honeydew, seeded

¹/₂ ripe cantaloupe, seeded

I cup fresh blueberries, washed

1. Draw a sharp wide-blade vegetable peeler along the length of the cut side of the honeydew, removing about 1¹/₂ cups of long wide strips. Pack the melon ribbons in a plastic container with a tight-fitting lid that is large enough for the honeydew and the cantaloupe.

2. Scoop out about 1 cup of cantaloupe balls with a melon baller. Add to the honeydew and refrigerate, tightly covered, until ready to pack for the picnic.

3. Add the blueberries to the melons.

4. To serve, divide the melons and blueberries between dessert dishes, arranging the honeydew on the bottom, topped with a layer of cantaloupe and a sprinkling of the blueberries.

Serves 2.

c o u n t d o w n   t o   s u c c e s s

I or 2 days ahead

➡ Prepare the pastry for the Walnut Tartlets

➡ Hard-cook the egg for the Salade Niçoise

➡ Prepare the Parsley Vinaigrette

➡ Make the Pears Poached in Red Wine

4 to 6 hours ahead

➡ Finish the Walnut Tartlets

➡ Prepare the Salad Niçoise through step 3

I to 3 hours ahead

➡ Cut the honeydew ribbons and make the cantaloupe balls

At the Picnic

➡ Assemble the Honeydew Ribbons and Cantaloupe with Blueberries

➡ Complete the Salade Niçoise

the allure of provence

This picnic menu reflects the heart of French country cuisine. Provence numbers among the most romantic places in the world where you can enjoy the pastoral beauty of quaint villages, vast fields of sunflowers, gorgeous vineyards, lush olive groves, and fragrant lavender fields.

What makes this region of the south of France so alluringly romantic is its appeal to the senses. Provence is blessed with an abundance of sunlight that makes the landscape shimmer. It was this "different light" that drew Vincent van Gogh and Paul Cézanne here to paint some of their most well-known masterpieces. But to really

indulge the senses, you must experience the culinary delights of Provence: simple, fresh ingredients and rustic fare that tantalize the palate, reminding you that good food and good friends are all you need. Robust garlic, a hint of extra-virgin olive oil,

the heady scent of basil, the mouthwatering flavor of fresh cheese, the aromas and bustle of outdoor village markets—this is Provence. To enjoy the allure of Provence in your own home, here are some of my favorite inspirations:

❱ Treat yourself to some of the beautiful fabrics of Provence: You can find gorgeous brightly colored tablecloths and napkins, quilted bags, even lamp shades, at Pierre Deux Fabrics, 870 Madison Avenue, New York, or visit the company's Web site at www.pierredeux.net.

❱ Decorate in the Provençal style: Store fruits and vegetables in wire baskets with wooden handles or hang framed prints of Provence, such as a lavender field or a quaint stone farmhouse. You can get ideas from home furnishings stores and catalogs such as *French Country Living*, 800-485-1302.

❱ Enjoy one of the many fine Provençal wines: No need to spend a fortune; one of the most enjoyable challenges of wine connoisseurs is to find a ten-dollar bottle of wine that tastes like it costs much more. Consult a local wine retailer for recommendations of wine from Provence or try one of the wine Web sites.

❱ Indulge your senses with fragrant lavender: Hang dried sprigs of lavender in your kitchen or enjoy lavender-scented soaps, lotions, and sachets.

❱ Cook a Provençal meal: Look for Provençal cookbooks in your local bookstore or library; add the classic herbes de Provence, available at most gourmet stores, to fish and meat dishes; or enjoy my Provençal Picnic *à Deux*, page 38.

Salade Niçoise

Featuring the classic Provençal ingredients of tuna, Niçoise olives, green beans, and baby red potatoes, Salade Niçoise is the salad of Nice, a city located on the Côte d'Azur. It's the most internationally known of all the regional salads and may indeed be the ultimate salad. A rustic country dish, not a fancy chef's concoction, it is a composed, rather than a tossed, salad. The original recipe was not made with mesclun (a mix of small-leafed greens), but very chic mesclun originated in this region, where it was originally the thinnings from the vegetable garden! Niçoise olives are tiny black brine-cured olives that are native to the area around Nice. You'll find them in jars at specialty food stores, and in many supermarkets, and at all olive bars. This recipe also calls for seeded English cucumber, which is available in better supermarkets; it often comes vacuum-wrapped.

4 whole baby red potatoes (about 2 inches
   in diameter)
I cup trimmed and halved fresh green beans
   (from about 4 ounces)
Parsley Vinaigrette (recipe follows)
¹/2 cup thinly sliced seeded English cucumber
One 6-ounce can light tuna,
   preferably packed in olive oil, drained
3 cups mesclun or shredded romaine lettuce,
   washed and spun dry
I ripe tomato, cored
I hard-cooked large egg, peeled
10 Niçoise olives

1. Put the potatoes in a medium saucepan and add water to cover by about 2 inches. Bring to a boil over high heat, salt the water, and boil the potatoes for 5 to 7 minutes, or until tender when pierced with a fork. Remove the potatoes with a slotted spoon and drain on paper towels (keep the water boiling for the next step). When cool enough to handle, cut the potatoes into quarters.

2. Add the green beans to the boiling water and cook for 3 to 5 minutes, or until crisp-tender. Drain them in a colander, refresh under cold running water to stop the cooking, and drain on paper towels.

3. Toss the potatoes with 1 teaspoon of the vinaigrette in a medium bowl. Transfer to a plastic container with a tight-fitting lid or a self-sealing plastic bag. Repeat with the green beans and cucumber, transferring each to a separate container. Toss the tuna with 1 tablespoon of the vinaigrette; transfer to a container. Refrigerate until ready

to pack for the picnic. Pack the mesclun, tomato, egg, and olives in separate containers or plastic bags and refrigerate.

4. To serve, arrange the mesclun in the center of dinner plates, dividing it evenly; drizzle each serving with about 1 teaspoon of the vinaigrette. Cut the tomato into wedges and quarter the egg. Place separate piles of the potatoes, green beans, cucumber, tomato, and egg around the mesclun. Put the tuna on top of the mesclun, drizzle the salad with the remaining vinaigrette, and garnish with the olives.

Serves 2.

Parsley Vinaigrette

1 small shallot, minced

3 tablespoons olive oil, preferably extra virgin

1 tablespoon plus 1 teaspoon red wine vinegar

1 tablespoon minced fresh parsley

1 teaspoon Dijon mustard

1/2 teaspoon salt

Large pinch of freshly ground pepper

Shake together all the ingredients in a jar with a tight-fitting lid until well blended.

Walnut Tartlets

Either separately or together, walnuts and honey are trademark flavors of Provence. Both are of an exceptional quality and figure largely in the region's desserts. These delectable tartlets are lovely served with coffee, tea, or Champagne. If you have a fear of pastry, simply skip rolling out the dough and press it directly into the tartlet pans; just make sure that it's a bit less than one-quarter inch thick.

Pastry

1/2 cup all-purpose flour

1 tablespoon sugar

Pinch of salt

3 tablespoons cold unsalted butter, cut into small pieces

1 large egg yolk

1 1/2 teaspoons ice water

Filling

1 cup walnut pieces

2 tablespoons unsalted butter, at room temperature

2 tablespoons sugar

2 tablespoons honey

3 tablespoons heavy cream

1. Make the pastry: Stir together the flour, sugar, and salt in a medium bowl with a fork. Cut in the butter with a pastry blender or two knives used scissor-fashion until the mixture resembles coarse meal. Stir together the egg yolk and water in a small bowl with a fork. Drizzle the yolk mixture over the flour mixture and stir with a fork just until combined. Press the dough together, divide it into 2 equal pieces, and shape each piece into a disk. Wrap each disk in waxed paper and refrigerate for at least 1 hour or up to 3 days.

2. Place a rack in the middle of the oven and preheat to 375°F. Have ready two 4- by 1-inch tartlet pans with removable bottoms.

3. Place one disk of dough on top of a floured sheet of waxed paper. Sprinkle the dough with flour and cover with another sheet of waxed paper. Roll the dough out to a 6-inch round, a scant $1/4$ inch thick. Peel off the top piece of waxed paper and invert the dough into a tartlet pan. Peel off and discard the second piece of waxed paper. Gently press the dough into bottom and against the side of the pan, patching the dough if necessary; trim the excess dough even with the edge of the pan. Repeat with the remaining disk. Refrigerate the shells for 15 minutes, or until firm. Line the tartlet shells with aluminum foil and fill with dry beans or rice. Place the shells on a baking sheet and bake for 10 minutes. Remove the foil and beans and bake for 6 or 7 minutes longer, or until the shells are firm and beginning to color.

4. Make the filling: Combine the walnuts, butter, sugar, and honey in a nonstick medium skillet over medium heat. Cook, stirring, for 4 to 5 minutes, or until the sugar mixture just begins to brown. Stir in the cream and bring to a boil; cook stirring, for 2 minutes longer, or until slightly thickened.

5. Evenly divide the filling between the tartlet shells. Bake for 10 minutes, or until filling is deep golden brown. Transfer the tartlets to a wire rack and cool to room temperature. Let stand at room temperature, covered, until ready to pack.

6. Tape the outside bottoms of the tartlet pans to the sides, wrap completely in foil, and pack separately in hard-sided plastic containers. Cushion them with paper towels to hold them in place.

7. To serve, remove the sides and bottoms of the tartlet pans and place the tartlets on small plates.

Serves 2.

packing tips

All of the dishes in this menu will keep safely at room temperature while traveling to the picnic, so a cooler isn't necessary. As a general rule, pack anything that might get crushed in hard-sided containers, and make certain they are leak-proof. Pack, keeping in mind how each food will be served.

■ If you feel sure the food won't be crushed, pack it in self-sealing plastic bags, and make sure not to pile anything on top.

■ Pack the vinaigrette in the jar you made it in.

■ If you want to keep a beverage, such as white wine, iced tea, or lemonade really cold, surround it with ice in leak-proof plastic bags, water frozen in milk cartons that have been taped shut, or frozen gel packs in a lightweight plastic or Styrofoam cooler.

Pears Poached in Red Wine

The sun-drenched climate of Provence is ideal for fruits. Here, use any variety of pear you like; I prefer Bartlett, which holds its shape well. The pears are poached ahead of time to completely absorb the color and flavor of the wine and look and taste their best. You might add a sprig of fresh basil to the poaching liquid— as they do in Provence—it makes the pears even more delicious.

3 cups dry red wine

$^1/_2$ cup packed brown sugar (light or dark)

4 thin lemon slices, seeded

1 3-inch cinnamon stick

2 firm-ripe pears

1 teaspoon pure vanilla extract

1. Bring the wine, sugar, lemon, and cinnamon to a boil in a medium saucepan. Reduce the heat to low; simmer 5 minutes.
2. Meanwhile, peel the pears, cut them lengthwise in half, and remove the cores. Add the pears to the simmering wine mixture; increase the heat to high and bring to a boil. Immediately reduce the heat to low and simmer, turning the pears occasionally, for 10 to 12 minutes, or until the pears are tender when pierced with a wooden skewer or pick.
3. Remove pears with a slotted spoon and place in a shallow dish in a single layer. Discard the lemon and cinnamon.
4. Increase the heat to high and boil the wine mixture for 10 minutes, or until it is reduced to about 2 cups. Transfer the liquid to a glass measure; let cool to room temperature, then stir in the vanilla. Pour the reduced wine mixture over the pears; cover and refrigerate for at least 1 day or up to 2 days, turning the pears occasionally.
5. To serve, transfer the pears to small bowls and drizzle each serving with about $^1/_4$ cup of the liquid.

Serves 2.

PICNIC *Checklist*

- ❑ Glasses
- ❑ Small dishes for the melon
- ❑ Dinner plates for the salad
- ❑ Small plates for the tartlets or small bowls for the pears
- ❑ Flatware (forks, spoons, and knives) for each course
- ❑ Small sharp paring knife to prepare the Salade Niçoise
- ❑ Tablecloth or handmade quilt and napkins
- ❑ Paper towels
- ❑ A corkscrew, if you're bringing wine or Champagne
- ❑ Coffee or tea in a thermos, cups, and milk and sugar or lemon, if desired
- ❑ Cold water for drinking, along with iced tea or lemonade
- ❑ Salt shaker and pepper mill
- ❑ Candles and wooden matches, if you're having an evening picnic
- ❑ Two damp washcloths, each scented with a drop of orange flower water or rose water and packed in plastic bags
- ❑ Garbage bag

Tips for a
PERFECT picnic

One of the great attractions of a picnic is its casual charm. You already have the ideal romantic setting of the great outdoors in your favor. You can have a picnic in the city, in the country, even in your own backyard. A picnic needn't take hours to prepare; all that's required is a little bit of planning:

▶ Choose a spot that offers some privacy. It needn't be completely secluded, just far enough away from the world that you can relax.

▶ Treat yourself to an old-fashioned picnic basket or transform one of your own baskets by lining it with pretty cloth napkins or tea towels.

▶ Make food the focal point but remember, simplicity is key. Forget about complicated meals that take hours to prepare. Pack some cheese and fresh bread, a pasta or rice salad or a dish that can be served cold, and fresh fruit for dessert. Or try my easy Provençal Picnic *à Deux* menu, page 38. Or you might just choose to raid your fridge and pantry for anything that can be packed in a container. Don't forget treats—your favorite cookies or brownies.

▶ Don't feel that you need to make everything yourself. Buy what you need if that will give the two of you more time together.

▶ Make your picnic special by bringing along a bottle of Champagne or fine wine and a pair of elegant glasses. Wrap the glasses in your cloth napkins for traveling. Don't get caught with a lovely bottle of wine and no corkscrew.

Write down a list of utensils you'll need so that you're sure to pack them.

▶ Use real dishes and silverware and take your salt shaker and pepper mill from your dining room table to create your "dining room al fresco."

▶ Bring a couple of small pillows so you can snooze after you eat or stare up at the clouds in the sky or the treetops and daydream.

Chapter 3

Romance
can be
SIMPLE

While grand gestures may sweep you off your feet, I believe that true romance is found more often in the simple pleasures of everyday life. Look around you: It's in the ritual of sharing a cup of coffee together in the morning or in the quick phone message that says I love you. It's that simple. My suggestion is that you make every day together a special one.

removing the "clutter" from YOUR *Relationship*

We all know what it feels like to have clutter in our homes, and I don't think many of us enjoy it. But just as your home can be filled with all manner of irrelevant things, so can your relationship. A general "tidying up" of the relationship can rid you of extraneous baggage that might be preventing you from being more romantic with each other.

❖ Think about giving your relationship a ritual "spring cleaning." First separately and then together with your partner, sit down and write out the issues you're facing, such as concerns or challenges regarding money, career, children, or in-laws. Putting things down on paper can help give you perspective. Talk together to separate the big issues from the smaller concerns. Consider several strategies for the big issues and agree on those you're most comfortable with. Make a commitment not to waste your energy on the small things.

❖ Let go of the past if you feel it's holding you back in your relationship; similarly, if you're constantly pre-occupied with the future, consciously focus on the here and now. Some people obsess about the past, others about the future—both can obscure the present, robbing you of time that you can fill with romance.

❖ Try to stay out of disputes outside of your relationship. For example, if your partner is having a bad time with his parents, offer him a sympathetic ear but steer clear of the dispute.

❖ Don't clog your relationship with hurtful words. If you can't say something constructive, it's better not to say anything at all.

creating your own
Romantic Rituals

*R*ituals can be the glue that holds couples together. I don't mean rituals in the solemn, ceremonial sense. A ritual is something that the two of you do together that you enjoy and that affirms your love for each other. For example, Bob always brings me flowers when he comes home from the office on Fridays. This has become one of our own personal rituals. Here are some ideas to inspire you to create your own romantic rituals:

❖ Bob and I consider Saturday night our date night, and we like to go out for dinner and a show, or sometimes we just go to the movies. Choose your own weekend date night and take turns surprising each other with theater tickets, dinner at a new restaurant, or other romantic surprise.

❖ At least once a week, set the table in a romantic way: with candles, a nosegay of fresh flowers, and your best dishes. This would make even Monday-night casserole feel like an occasion!

❖ Keep a framed photograph of the two of you on your bedside table, and make it a

regular ritual to put a different picture in the frame. Take turns choosing which one to feature.

❖ Revisit a spot that has made you happy in the past. There's something very romantic about going back to the place where your partner proposed.

❖ Share a few moments each week reading a romantic or inspirational message to your love. It could be something you've written or a quote or story that warmed your heart. Look for ideas during the week. Something might capture your attention in a magazine in the doctor's waiting room or in an interview on the radio, or you might be inspired by a song you hear or a beautiful sunset you catch in your rearview mirror.

❖ I know of someone whose husband makes it his own ritual, at a different time each day, to coyly say to his wife, "Have I told you I love you yet today?" She never knows when he's going to say it, but it makes her smile every time. She always says, "No," and waits for those three magic words.

❖ Spend at least a few minutes together talking in bed before you go to sleep. This is no time to tussle over household or work issues; share thoughts and feelings that will calm your spirit and bring you sweet dreams.

sending
Romantic Messages

I believe that you should never take for granted that your partner knows he is loved. Tell him every day, in different ways, how important he is to you. Creating your own romantic messages is a fun challenge. Here are a handful of thought starters:

❖ Call your spouse when you know he's not at work, for example, just after he leaves the house in the morning, and leave him a message telling him that you miss him already.

❖ Call a local radio station and request a song to be dedicated to your love. Choose a song that has a special meaning for both of you, and make sure your partner is listening to the radio program at the right time.

❖ For fun, send him an online greeting card. There are many Web sites that offer this service.

❖ Buy him a novel you know he'll love, and write little romantic messages on self-adhesive notes and place them on random pages throughout the book.

The Incurable Romantic
love letters

Perhaps it's because writing was my very first love that writing love letters has always played an important role in my relationship with Bob. And you don't need to be a pro to put ink to paper; you just need to be honest about what's in your heart. Here are my recommendations for writing love letters:

▶ Don't be shy. Think of a love letter as an opportunity to say things that might make you blush or become tongue-tied in person.

▶ Use a beautiful, heavy paper for your letter. You might also want to use a favorite pen that writes in an unusual ink to mark the letter as special.

▶ Handwriting your letter gives it a loving, personal touch that can't be equaled by a computer!

▶ You might use the letter to describe a special day the two of you spent together or another special event of significance to your relationship. It's also a chance to tell your partner exactly what you love about him!

▶ Seal your letter with a wax seal, available from many stationers. Choose

a romantic seal, such as a heart motif, or the Chinese character for the word "love."

▶ Buy a book of historic love letters. Not only can you read them aloud to each other, but you can use them as an inspiration for writing your own missives. I recommend Antonia Fraser's *Love Letters*, which contains letters from Napoleon to Josephine, Winston Churchill to his wife Clementine, Thomas Jefferson to Maria Cosway, Sir Thomas More to Margaret Roper. It's a marvelous anthology that makes a great gift, also.

▶ If your spouse is traveling on business, send a love letter ahead of time to his hotel so it will be waiting for him when he arrives.

▶ While writing a love letter is a wonderful way to mark a special occasion, don't wait for a big event to put pen to paper. Receiving a love letter makes any day special!

▶ Gather together your love letters, wrap them in ribbon, and store them in a special box. Be sure to read them again and again, and read them aloud to each other.

the ART of *Communication*

As a novelist, I have a special interest in how people communicate. Whenever I create a character, I base the way he or she speaks, at least in part, on conversations I've heard—or sometimes overheard! Perhaps this has given me an ear for how to communicate—and how not to. Let me share what I've learned.

✤ Communication involves listening as well as speaking. One of my favorite old sayings is that we have two ears and one mouth because we're supposed to listen twice as much as we talk! Active listening doesn't mean waiting until your partner has said his piece before you launch into all the points you want to make; it means acknowledging and showing you under-stand what your partner is saying to you. One way to do this is to say, "I think what you're saying is…" and repeat the main points he's made. This gives him a chance to correct you or restate his point if he thinks you've misunderstood.

✤ Nonverbal cues, such as eye contact and posture, generally reflect your level of interest and engagement in a conversa-tion. Defensively crossing your arms over

your chest, for example, means you're not really listening to what your partner is saying or you don't want to be listening. More positive signals include keeping your body turned toward your partner's, not turned away at an angle, or leaning slightly forward toward your partner, remaining calm rather than fidgeting, and maintaining direct eye contact.

✤ Find a private space to talk openly together, somewhere you don't fear being overheard. If you can't find it in the house, take a walk together.

✤ If something he does bothers you, bring it up gently but directly. There's no need to say something cold like: "I really hate it when you…" That will cut off the conversa-tion. Start out instead by saying: "It makes

the romantic countryside of yorkshire

Since I have written about Yorkshire in many of my novels, my readers have become very familiar with this northern corner of England. It is very beautiful with its high-flung fells, rolling moors covered with purple heather in August and September, and the verdant dales that stretch across half the county, which happens to be the largest in England.

The green fields of the dales are crisscrossed with low stone walls built by hand by the crofters, who balance stones so well, no cement is needed to secure them. Here roam sheep, which thrive on the short, sweet grass and limestone water of the district and which gave rise to Yorkshire's woolen industry: In Bradford the sheep's wool is woven into cloth; in Leeds the cloth is made into ready-to-wear clothing. My mother came from the cathedral town of Ripon, in the middle of the dales, and this beautiful old city is a favorite of mine, with its cobblestone streets, great cathedral, and the extraordinary ruins of Fountains Abbey.

In particular, I love going to Middleham, just a few miles from Ripon. Here, on top of the windswept moors, are the ruins of the once-great Middleham Castle, home of Richard Neville, the Earl of Warwick, also known as the Kingmaker, since he put Edward IV on the throne of England at the end of the Wars of the Roses. I set a romantic Christmas scene in Middleham in my novel *Where You Belong*. To me, there is nothing more romantic than those empty, rolling moors, stretching as far as the eye can see, windswept under cloudy, often thunderous skies. I also find the "Gallops" in Middleham another romantic spot. It is here every morning at six o'clock that the stable boys bring the racehorses out to gallop across the moors at the edge of the horizon. Middleham has many well-known racing stables where some of the most renowned racehorses have been trained over the years. Here are some ways to enjoy the romance of Yorkshire and British history:

▶ Read about the periods in history that fascinate you. In English history, I think the Wars of the Roses, between the House of York, represented

by the white rose, and the House of Lancaster, symbolized by the red rose, is one of the most compelling. My favorite period is that of the Tudors, though, from the extraordinary Henry VIII to his daughter Elizabeth I.

❯ Watch period films. There are many fascinating films about Elizabeth I, for example, from *Elizabeth and Essex*, with Bette Davis in the title role, to the more recent *Elizabeth*, starring Cate Blanchett. However, the latter is historically *incorrect*. Elizabeth was never betrayed by Robert Dudley, Earl of Leicester, and remained close to him until his death. As long as he lived they were inseparable.

❯ Horses are a passion in Yorkshire. Visit a stable to go riding with your partner or take an introductory lesson if you're new to the horse world. Attend a horse show or race, or watch one of the famous horse races that are televised: the Kentucky Derby, Preakness, and Belmont Stakes.

❯ For an unforgettable, romantic vacation, I recommend taking a castle tour of Great Britain. It has many beautiful palaces, including Buckingham Palace in London, one of the Queen's residences. If you love ruined castles, as I do, Caerphilly Castle in Wales and Dunluce Castle in Northern Ireland are among the most majestic, in addition to Middleham Castle. Then there is Windsor Castle, where the Queen still lives.

❯ Partake of the delightful English ritual of afternoon tea. (See "The Romantic Gourmet: The Ritual of Afternoon Tea," page 56, and the menu, "An Old-Fashioned Yorkshire Tea for Two," page 58, for ideas.)

me feel uncomfortable when… [fill in the blank]. Could we talk about it?"

♣ Use the classic "I" statements, that is, statements that begin with "I" rather than "You." Saying "You always do X" won't foster good communication; your partner may just feel attacked. Saying "It makes me feel upset when you X" opens the door to discussing a problem.

♣ Interruptions kill communication. If you're having a difficult discussion, it's a good idea to let your spouse speak without interruption until he's said his piece. Only then do you respond. Expect the same from him.

♣ Timing is everything. Try not to approach your partner for an important talk when he is engaged in another activity. If he's busy, tell him there's something you'd like to talk about and ask when a good time would be.

♣ Be very conscious of your tone. Content's one thing, but delivery can also make or break successful communication. Women are notorious for unknowingly adopting an annoying, cloying, or sarcastic tone of voice, or raising their pitch when upset or angry. Speak in a level manner.

the POWER of *Forgiveness*

Forgiveness can be one of the greatest gifts you give your partner. I've learned that it takes a lot of love, acceptance, and maturity in order to forgive sincerely. You need to operate from a position of strength to forgive—my suggestions below aren't for the faint of heart!

❖ Be the first one to take the first step to make amends after an argument or fight. Even if you're convinced that you're not the one "at fault," remember that no one can argue by himself. Letting go of a grudge will give you a sense of freedom and peace.

❖ Let go of any anger you might be holding onto about something that your partner did in the past. Write it down and shred it if that helps, but don't let it affect the relationship the two of you have now.

❖ Patch up old wounds with your husband's family. If the hurt goes too deep, allow yourself to step back from the relationship emotionally,

but don't keep fighting a draining, never-ending battle with them that puts your partner in the middle.

❖ Don't play the "If you hadn't done X, Y wouldn't have happened" game. We're not psychic, so we cannot envision what every consequence of our actions will be.

❖ Accept that everyone has certain foibles, traits that aren't always lovable but are nonetheless part of one's personality. If your partner is cranky in the morning, understand that this has nothing to do with you and let it go. Slip out of bed early and save your together time for later.

❖ Remember a time when you were forgiven and how much better you felt. See if you can look beyond your partner's anger or actions for a clue, such as acting out of ignorance, fear, or pain, that might shed light on the situation.

❖ Don't forget to forgive yourself when things don't go the way you want them to. Accept that some things are beyond your control, too.

❖ Don't make silent demands and then sulk when they're not met. Say it aloud, so he knows what you want.

SECRETS to love: *Respect*

I think that in order to love someone, you must first respect him and that respect must be tended to for the duration of the relationship. A romantic partnership is a relationship between equals— I believe it's virtually impossible to have a successful relationship, let alone a romantic one, with someone you don't respect as an equal. Respect is a form of honoring a person and his individuality, and it's so important that it's part of the traditional wedding vows ("love and honor").

Respect means holding your partner in a position of high regard and showing that you believe he is genuinely worthy. This can be done in many ways, but an important one is to be wholly attentive to him when you listen. If he's telling you a story, don't interrupt. When he's done, ask him, "Then what happened?" or "I think the part about X was so interesting. What do you think?" Here are some suggestions that can help deepen your respect for your lover:

✤ *Respect his ideas and opinions.* Don't expect that the two of you will agree on every-thing—you're lovers, not Siamese twins! Agree to disagree about certain issues, such as politics or what constitutes great art. As long as you agree on core values, such as how to raise your family, there's a lot of room to debate everything else.

✤ *Respect his individuality.* You fell in love with him the way he is; don't try to change him now. Trying to "convert" your partner to your way of doing things means you're convinced that your ways are "right" while his are "wrong"—the opposite of respect. Focus your efforts instead on constructively navigating the areas where you differ in order to find solutions or the "middle road." Compromise is key to a successful relationship.

✤ *Respect his accomplishments.* Be proud of your spouse for what he's achieved in his family life, at work, within your community, or in his leisure activities. Give him lots of positive feedback for these accomplishments.

✤ *Respect his goals and dreams.* Your partner's dreams won't all be the same as yours, but your support for them should be unwavering. Respecting him means honoring his ambitions. Offer him unconditional support in whatever he does, and help him realize his dreams. This is what having a relationship is about.

The Ritual of
afternoon TEA

While afternoon tea is one of England's most charming rituals, tea cultivation actually began in China some four thou-sand years ago. Europeans didn't taste tea until the seventeenth century, but the British quickly developed a fondness for it. They loved it so much that they creat-ed a meal just to enjoy tea, called high tea. Served in the late afternoon around five o'clock, high tea is a real meal with such dishes as pork pie, veal pie, trifle dessert, and other foods. Afternoon tea, which is usually served at four, is com-posed of small tea sandwiches, cakes, and scones with jam. For many years, having tea was a habit that only the rich could afford since tea leaves were so expen-sive, but in the Victorian era, when India became part of the British Empire, tea became widely accessible.

▌ Different climates and soils create very different flavors in the leaves. Black tea is perhaps the best known, with varieties that include English Breakfast, Darjeeling, and Orange Pekoe. Other types include oolong and green tea, long popular in Asia and recently gaining new fans worldwide because of the health benefits derived from its antioxidant compounds.

▌ Public teahouses, sometimes called tearooms, are still popular in England. Some of the most famous are Shepherds

in Chichester, Waterstone's in Bath, Betty's Cafe in Harrogate, and Politico's in London, the latter part of a famous bookstore. In London, I love afternoon tea at the Ritz Hotel. One of the most elegant tearooms in Paris is Ladurée. In New York, the Stanhope Hotel, just across from the Metropolitan Museum of Art, serves tea, as does the Plaza Hotel, one of my favorites. If you live in a large city, there may be a hotel and some restaurants that offer afternoon tea. This can be a luxurious treat for the two of you when you want to splurge (though it's much less expensive than a dinner out!).

◗ Students at Cambridge University have taken their tea at Orchard House for over a century. One of my favorite poets, Rupert Brooke, lived here while he was an undergraduate. Orchard House has an indoor pavilion where tea is served, though in fine weather many people will stroll out with their tea to the adjoining orchard, which is filled with apple, plum, and pear trees.

◗ Americans have contributed their own innovations to tea.

Both the invention of tea bags and the custom of drinking iced tea hail from the United States.

◗ Afternoon tea makes a lovely weekly or monthly ritual. Having tea every Sunday afternoon is a wonderful way to cap off the week.

◗ While I adore tea, I know it's not everyone's drink of choice. Afternoon "tea" can be served with coffee or cocoa, too, if that's what your spouse prefers.

The Right Way to Make a Pot of Tea

The English are very particular about how to prepare a "proper" cup of tea. First, know that it's made in the pot, not the cup. To begin, heat the teapot with boiling water: Swirl the water around the teapot and then discard before adding loose tea or tea bags. If you use loose tea, scoop one teaspoon of tea for each person plus "one for the pot" into a tea infuser, or loose in the pot if you prefer. If you use tea bags, place one tea bag per cup of water in the pot. Add boiling water to the pot and let the tea steep for five minutes. Once the tea is ready, add a little milk to the teacup first, if you prefer, then pour. Sugar is optional, of course. Or you can serve black and add a slice of lemon.

old-fashioned yorkshire tea for two

Emma, the dynamic matriarch in my first novel, A Woman of Substance, *enjoys the daily ritual of afternoon tea at Pennistone Royal, her house in Yorkshire. Scones, a must for a traditional tea, are served with a choice of spreads including butter and strawberry jam. To qualify as a cream tea, the scones are served with clotted cream, also known as Devon cream. Clotted cream is a wonderfully thick, rich reduction made by separating the cream off the milk and then gently simmering it until it "clots." Imported from England, clotted cream is usually sold in small glass jars at gourmet food stores and better supermarkets. For something different, you might also try a rum butter, prepared by beating a half stick of soft unsalted butter with about one-quarter cup of light brown sugar, a pinch each of ground allspice and cinnamon, and a couple of teaspoons of dark rum. It's delicious and it lasts, tightly covered, in your refrigerator for up to two months.*

Some of my favorite teas for afternoon tea include: English breakfast, Irish breakfast, or Ceylon orange pekoe from Twinings or Taylor's of Harrogate. I enjoy rosehip or chamomile from Pompadour for other meals. If you don't want to make English biscuits, you can buy them. I'm partial to Cadbury Chocolate Fingers. Here are some suggestions to make your tea menu memorable:

❖ Pick your location; you needn't use the dining room. Afternoon tea is lovely served on a deck or patio, in the living room with a fire blazing, or the bedroom.

❖ Set the table with a lace tablecloth and cloth napkins. Serve the tea in a silver or fine china teapot. If you don't have a complete tea set, don't worry. Create your own mix and match tea set with cups and saucers purchased from different antique shops. Remember, you only need two!

❖ Don't forget sugar cubes and small tongs so you can ask your love, "One lump or two?"

❖ The Victorians popularized "The Language of Flowers," a tradition in which individual flowers were believed to express a certain message or sentiment (see "A World of Love in Flowers," page 80, for tips). Fill a vase with a bouquet that symbolizes your feelings about your partner. Neatly print the bouquet's meaning on a note card placed next to the vase. ❖ During the Victorian era, inviting a suitor to tea was part of the courting process. Send your partner a handwritten invitation. You can leave the invitation on his pillow, mail it, or, if you live in a city, have a messenger service hand deliver it, as they did in Victorian times (only then, of course, they traveled on horseback—not bicycle). ❖ Use music to set a romantic mood. I love the piano music of twentieth-century Russian composer and pianist Rachmaninoff, who wrote in the style of the late nineteenth-century Romantic composers. His music is filled with emotional conflict, at times haunting, at times gentle and passionate. You might try Piano Concerto No. 1 in F-Sharp Minor, Op. 1.; Piano Concerto No. 2 in C Minor, Op. 18; and *Rhapsody on a Theme of Paganini.*

Menu

Warm Scones with Strawberry Jam and Devon Cream

Cucumber, Smoked Salmon, and Tomato Tea Sandwiches

Dainty Rich Butter Cookies (English Biscuits)

Yorkshire Madeira Cake

Warm Scones with Strawberry Jam and Devon Cream

No matter what you choose to serve with your scones, they are best enjoyed warm. If you have leftovers, just pop them in a self-sealing plastic bag and freeze. Then you simply thaw them and gently reheat in a toaster oven for an almost-instant breakfast.

^{1}/$_3$ cup heavy cream

1 large egg white

1 teaspoon finely grated lemon zest

1 cup all-purpose flour

2 tablespoons light brown sugar

1^1/$_2$ teaspoons baking powder

Pinch of salt

2 tablespoons cold unsalted butter, cut into small pieces

Clotted cream, strawberry jam, and/or soft unsalted butter and marmalade, for serving

1. Position a rack in the middle of the oven and preheat to 375°F.

2. Whisk together the cream, egg white, and lemon zest in a small bowl. Combine the flour, brown sugar, baking powder, and salt in a large bowl, using your fingers to break up the brown sugar. Cut the butter into the dry ingredients with a pastry blender or two knives used scissor-fashion until the mixture resembles coarse meal. Slowly pour the cream mixture into the dry ingredients and stir with a fork just until a dough forms (do not overmix).

3. Knead the dough about 8 times, with lightly floured hands, in the bowl, just until it comes together. On a lightly floured surface, form the dough into a 6-inch disk about $1/2$ inch thick. Transfer the disk to an ungreased baking sheet and cut into 8 wedges with a floured knife. Separate the wedges slightly.

4. Bake the scones for 22 to 25 minutes, until golden brown. Transfer the scones to a wire rack to cool slightly. Serve warm with clotted cream, strawberry jam, and/or soft unsalted butter and marmalade.

Makes 8 small scones.

Cucumber, Smoked Salmon, and Tomato Tea Sandwiches

Perfectly English and perfectly delicious, tea sandwiches are an absolute necessity for any tea party. You can use this recipe to create a mixed platter with a variety of fillings and breads. Egg salad is also a popular tea sandwich filling. Follow the directions below using your favorite egg salad recipe, to add more variety to your platter, if you wish. This recipe calls for cutting the sandwiches into quarters and halves; however, you may prefer to cut them into more traditional "fingers"—narrow rectangles.

English (seedless) cucumbers are available in better supermarkets and usually come vacuum-wrapped. The purist wouldn't do this, but if you want to fancy up the cucumber sandwiches, add a few delicate fresh dill sprigs or mint leaves. Or add a few watercress sprigs to the tomato sandwiches, if you like.

Note: If you plan to make these sandwiches ahead of time, line a 9-inch square baking pan with barely damp paper towels. Place the tea sandwiches in the pan; cover with plastic wrap, top with damp paper towels to keep the bread from drying out, and cover the pan tightly with plastic wrap. Refrigerate until ready to serve.

Cucumber Tea Sandwiches

One 3-inch length English (seedless) cucumber

1/4 teaspoon salt

4 very thin slices white bread, crusts removed

2 tablespoons unsalted butter, at room
temperature

Fresh dill sprigs or mint leaves (optional)

Smoked Salmon Tea Sandwiches

8 very thin slices whole wheat or
brown bread, crusts removed

3 tablespoons unsalted butter, at room
temperature

4 ounces very thinly sliced smoked salmon

Tomato Tea Sandwiches

2 small ripe tomatoes (about 3 ounces each)

2 very thin slices whole wheat bread,
crusts removed

2 very thin slices white bread, crusts removed

2 tablespoons unsalted butter, at room
temperature

Salt and freshly ground pepper

1. Make the cucumber sandwiches: Peel the
cucumber and thinly slice. (If making the
sandwiches ahead, put the cucumber slices
in a colander set over a bowl. Sprinkle
with the salt and toss to coat. Let stand
at room temperature for 30 minutes,
stirring occasionally. Dry the cucumber
on paper towels.)

2. Spread one side of each bread slice with
butter. Arrange the cucumber on 2 of
the bread slices; place 1 mint leaf in each
quarter of the sandwich, if desired. Top
with the remaining bread. Cut each
sandwich diagonally into quarters.

3. Make the smoked salmon sandwiches:
Spread one side of each bread slice
with butter. Arrange the salmon on
4 of the bread slices, trimming the
salmon to fit if necessary. Top with
the remaining bread. Cut each sandwich
into two rectangles.

4. Make the tomato sandwiches: Cut the
tomatoes into 8 very thin slices. Spread
one side of each slice of bread with the
butter. Arrange the tomatoes on the
whole wheat bread, and season with salt
and pepper. Top with remaining bread.
Cut each sandwich into four squares.

Makes 24 tea sandwiches.

Dainty Rich Butter Cookies
(English Biscuits)

Your sweetheart will love these cookies: They're simple, rich, and buttery—and the heart shape is ideal for a romantic tea. They can be stored for a day in an airtight container or frozen until you plan to serve them. Most important is to roll the dough out to an even thickness so the cookies bake evenly.

4 tablespoons (1/2 stick) unsalted butter,
   at room temperature
2 tablespoons granulated sugar
2 tablespoons light brown sugar
1 large egg yolk
1/2 teaspoon pure vanilla extract
1/2 cup all-purpose flour
Pinch of salt

1. Cream the butter with the sugars in a medium bowl with an electric mixer on medium speed for 2 minutes, or until very light and fluffy. Add the egg yolk and vanilla and beat until blended. Reduce the speed to very low. Add the flour and salt, mixing just until blended; do not overmix. Shape the dough into a disk, wrap in waxed paper, and refrigerate until firm, at least 4 hours or overnight.

2. Position a rack in the middle of the oven and preheat to 350°F. Lightly butter a large baking sheet.

3. On a floured surface, with a floured rolling pin, roll the dough out until 1/4 inch thick. Cut out cookies with a floured 3-inch heart-shaped cutter; transfer the cookies to the prepared baking sheet, spacing them about 1 inch apart. Repeat with the remaining dough, rerolling the scraps.

4. Bake for 8 to 10 minutes, until the edges are light golden brown. Transfer the cookies to a wire rack to cool completely. Store in an airtight container for up to 1 day or freeze for up to a month.

Makes 16 cookies.

c o u n t d o w n   t o   s u c c e s s

3 or More Days Ahead
➡ Make the Dainty Rich Butter Cookies and freeze

2 Days Ahead
➡ Make the Yorkshire Madeira Cake

4 Hours Ahead
➡ Make the Cucumber, Smoked Salmon, and Tomato Tea Sandwiches

30 Minutes Ahead
➡ Make the Warm Cream Scones

Yorkshire Madeira Cake

Originally the traditional accompaniment to a glass of Madeira, this rich but simple pound cake, sprinkled with candied lemon peel partway through baking, is a classic English favorite. Measuring the flour correctly is crucial. Stir flour in canister, spoon it into measuring cup, then level off top with the straight side of a table knife. Sift flour after measuring, not before. Here, sifting the flour twice makes for the perfect crumb. If you don't want to make candied lemon zest, you can purchase it. It usually comes chopped: you'll need 2 tablespoons.

2 cups all-purpose flour, sifted
Pinch of salt
1 cup (2 sticks) unsalted butter, at room
   temperature
3/4 cup sugar
4 large eggs
Candied Lemon Zest, optional (recipe follows)

1. Position a rack in the middle of the oven and preheat to 350°F. Butter an 8 1/2-by 4 1/2- by 2 1/2-inch loaf pan. Dust the pan with flour, shaking out the excess.

2. Whisk together the flour and salt in a medium bowl.

3. Beat the butter and sugar in a large deep bowl with an electric mixer on medium-high speed for about 3 minutes, or until very light and fluffy. Add the eggs, one at a time, beating well after each addition. Sift in the dry ingredients and fold in with a whisk.

4. Transfer the batter to the prepared pan; smooth the top with a rubber spatula, mounding it slightly in the center. Bake for 1 hour. Sprinkle the cake with the Candied Lemon Zest, if using, and bake for 15 minutes longer, or just until a wooden pick inserted in the center comes out clean.

5. Completely cool the cake in the pan on a wire rack. Run a table knife around the edge of the pan and invert the cake onto a plate. Cut into slices and serve. Can be made up to 2 days ahead. Store, completely cooled and tightly wrapped, at room temperature.

Makes one loaf.

Candied Lemon Zest

Remove the zest from 1 medium lemon with a vegetable peeler. Scrape away any white pith with a knife. Cut the strips into needle-thin strips. Place the zest in a medium saucepan, cover with cold water, and bring to a boil over high heat. Boil for 1 minute, transfer to a strainer, and rinse under cold running water. Return the zest to the same saucepan and repeat the process. Combine 3 tablespoons sugar and 3 tablespoons water in a small saucepan and bring to a boil over medium heat. Stir in lemon zest, reduce heat to low, and simmer, stirring occasionally, for 4 minutes, or until translucent. Remove zest from syrup with a slotted spoon.

finding
Romance
EVERY day

Romance isn't just for the special occasions on your calendar—it's what makes any time you have together special. Celebrate what you have! Time together balanced with time apart, along with healthy doses of trust and humor, will make your every day sparkle. It's time to enjoy the here and now.

celebrating your *Love* EVERY day

We live in a culture that plans toward special occasions, and yet so often does not appreciate the beauty of living together in love day after day. While I must admit that I'm as fond of Valentine's Day as anyone, I have never believed in storing up romantic moments just for the "big days" in life. Special occasions, while tremendously important, account for so little of the time that we spend with our lover or spouse. Here's how to start enjoying what you share each and every day:

❖ Think about what you particularly enjoy about the special days through the year that you celebrate together, such as your wedding anniversary. Do you set aside time to spend together, cook a special meal, or write a love letter? Whatever it is, identify it and bring more of it into the rest of your days.

❖ Toast each other when you sit down to dinner. You needn't break out the bubbly or even wine; you could just as easily be drinking water or tea. But tell each other something you love about the other person or about your life together, and drink to it.

❖ Use the power of touch every day. There is no such thing as a day that you don't have time to kiss each other good-bye before leaving the house in the morning or again upon reuniting at the end of the day. And a warm hug or back rub at any time of day is always appreciated.

The Incurable Romantic
love poems

There is a timeless quality to romantic poetry. I find that even if the language sounds different to our ears, the heartfelt sentiment still carries through loud and clear. Many people feel perhaps a little bit afraid of poetry, thinking of it as something they had to memorize in school and would rather forget about. Some people think that they don't understand poetry or that they would sound silly reading it aloud. But it can be a wonderful discovery to find that a poet writing two hundred or more years ago can so perfectly express what we are feeling in our own souls. Start by reading some poetry and deciding what you like—poets are very different, just like novelists. Here are some ways for you and your partner to discover and enjoy romantic poetry:

▶ My favorite poets are Lord Byron, Emily Brontë, Elizabeth Barrett Browning, and Rupert Brooke. Byron's "She Walks in Beauty" still touches me deeply. Buy an anthology of poetry and leaf through it together for inspiration.

▶ Read poems aloud to each other. Shakespeare's sonnets can be enjoyed alone, but they are truly magical when the words are given a voice. Sit outside on a beautiful day to read Sonnet 18 to your love: "Shall I compare thee to a summer's day?" The setting will drive home the romance of the words.

▶ Shop in secondhand bookstores or at auctions for older editions of books of poetry. These are often clothbound, and they may even have pen-and-ink or watercolor illustrations. The books look romantic themselves, and the process of searching can be an adventure.

▶ Find a poem that really resonates in your heart and memorize it line by line. Surprise your partner by reciting it when you're alone together.

▶ Copy out a favorite poem by hand and tuck it into your partner's briefcase. He'll come upon it when he least expects it. If you can fit the words inside a blank card with a romantic painting or photograph on the front, all the better!

▶ Poetry isn't just the classics. Haiku is a form of poetry, for example. Look for a book of haiku at the library or bookstore. Check the Internet too. There are numerous Web sites that offer a sampling of haiku. Find one that touches your heart and share it with your partner.

✤ Don't save the camera just for holiday time. Take candid pictures of your everyday life together: gardening, painting a room, cooking in the kitchen. Better still, set the camera on an automatic timer and pose together. Some of these photos might seem comic, but the warmth of the moment will be caught forever. Add them to your memory book or album, and frame at least one.

✤ Do something thoughtful for your partner every day. Consideration is in the small gestures, such as bringing your partner a cup of coffee or a snack when he's working on something at home, or leaving a chocolate "kiss" for him on his pillow at bedtime.

✤ Set something aside each day to share with your spouse. It might be an article in the newspaper you thought was funny or interesting, a tidbit you saw on a Web site, or even a story you heard from a friend or on the radio.

How not to take your Partner for *Granted*

It's wonderful knowing that your partner will always be there for you. But it can also be a slippery slope to taking him for granted. Bob and I are careful about listening to each other—we often talk on the phone four times a day! Really listening to each other and showing appreciation are essential to avoiding one partner's risk of feeling taken for granted.

✤ Tell your husband that you love him every single day. It's one of my strongest beliefs that you should never let a day go by without saying these magic words.

❖ Remember the old saying "Don't kick the cat." In other words, don't take out your anger or frustration over an outside situation on your partner. He's your support system, not your punching bag.

❖ Be generous with your compliments. To me, my husband's eyes are as soulful as they were on the day we first met, and I like to tell him so. This isn't flattery; these words virtually flow at the start of a relationship, but it's easy to forget to say them later. Just remember, there's no one in this world who doesn't relish a sincere compliment, especially your own partner.

❖ Be honest if you're feeling stressed or under the weather. Saying "I've had a terrible day" or "I'm so angry about…" is important to head off pointless arguments. Instead of taking out whatever's wrong on

each other, treat your love with TLC. And if you're still in a mood, at least your partner will know not to take it personally.

❖ Let your spontaneous side show through. Taking someone for granted can be the result of getting stuck in a bad routine. Breaking the routine—by meeting him after work if that's something you wouldn't normally do—lets more romance into your life.

❖ Let your love see you at your best. It's ironic to me that we dress up to meet with strangers and yet think nothing of letting our appearance go when we are around our nearest and dearest. You don't have to dress as if you're going to appear on prime time television, but wearing attractive colors, well-fitting clothes, and keeping a tidy appearance are important.

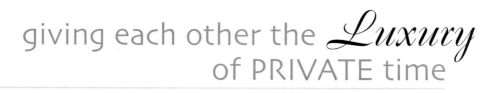

giving each other the *Luxury* of PRIVATE time

While I love spending time with Bob, it's vitally important that we have time apart as well. Does that sound unromantic? It's anything but. Time apart lets you recharge yourselves, and this in turn revitalizes the relationship. Here are some ideas:

❖ Know that you and your love will want to spend your private time differently. You may need the company of your girlfriends, while your husband might crave some quiet time to putter around the house. Try not to judge, and try not to "suggest" what your partner should do. Let "To each his own" be your mantra.

❖ Set some boundaries for your time apart. One partner should not be out enjoying time alone while the other is home minding the kids every night. You need to be fair and give each other equal opportunity to enjoy time away.

❖ If you're dying to do something like go to the ballet and your partner has no interest, let him off the hook and attend the performance alone or with a friend. While it's reasonable to expect your partner to give your interests a try, it's not right to expect him to go and grind his teeth.

❖ Help out wherever you can with your partner's private-time activities. If he's planning to host a Super Bowl party for his friends, help him stock the house with food and drink before escaping for the afternoon yourself.

❖ Pamper yourself during some of your own private time by recharging at a salon or day spa—a ritual with a precedent in ancient mythology. According to the Greeks, at a certain time each year, the goddess Hera would go into a retreat that included a special bath that restored her youth. When she emerged from seclusion, her husband, Zeus, would fall in love with her all over again.

❖ Always, always, sit down together when you get home and relate your experiences apart. The best thing about spending time apart is that it makes you appreciate each other all the more. Now you're ready to take on the world together.

Baci da Venezia—Kisses from Venice

La Serenissima (Most Serene), as the city is called, holds everyone in its spell. In between visits, I also enjoy the evocative paintings of Venice by the great British artist J. M. W. Turner, which capture the city in such wonderful light. Sixteenth-century artists such as Tintoretto, Tiziano (also known as Titian) and Veronese created great works of art here, and the architecture of Andrea Palladio is a legacy to Venice.

Venice, built on stilts on 117 islands separated by nearly two hundred small canals, dates back to the fifth century, when people took refuge there from barbarian invasions. When I do visit, I enjoy shopping for unusual

stationery, silk scarves, and Venetian glass, hand-blown on the adjacent island of Murano. I collect Venetian wineglasses, so I am always on the lookout, especially for those that are old.

Once in Venice, Bob bought me a gold ring of tiny intersecting diamond hearts and gave it to me when we were having dinner at the famous Harry's Bar, the most renowned restaurant on the Piazza de San Marco, which Napoleon called "the finest drawing room in Europe." Later, we went back to our hotel, the Cipriani in Guidecca, on a gondola, and there was a full moon—the most romantic way to see Venice. Here are some ideas to help you experience the magic of Venice:

❱ Create your own "gondola" ride. Find a lake, canal, or river in your area with canoes or rowboats to rent. You might plan your outing for dusk, when the light is especially beautiful. Enjoy the serenity of the quiet water and the gentle lapping sound of the oars cutting through the water.

❱ Catch Venice on film: *Summertime*, starring Katherine Hepburn; *The Wings of the Dove*, based on the Henry James novel; and *A Little Romance*, with Laurence Olivier and a young Diane Lane. The young couple in the last movie play out the romantic legend of kissing under the Bridge of Sighs in a gondola at the stroke of midnight to "seal" their everlasting love. Also, Bob filmed the movie based on my book *A Secret Affair* in Venice. It was shown on CBS, so look for it in reruns.

❱ Enjoy a delicious *bellini* cocktail, the ever-popular Champagne and peach nectar mix from the famous Harry's Bar in Venice.

the GIFT of *Laughter*

I love a good laugh. Who doesn't? And I must admit, Bob is the one who makes me laugh the most—he has a great dry sense of humor. Laughter is like a soothing balm: It restores your equilibrium and makes the world seem like a much more manageable place. Sharing laughter with your love is not only great fun, it's also something that makes your relationship stronger. You needn't be a great comedian, just keep these ideas in mind:

❖ Tell your spouse a funny story about something silly you've done. There is something incredibly charming and confident about a person who can lightly poke fun at herself.

❖ Buy a book written by your favorite comedian and read out loud from it when you and your partner need a good laugh.

❖ Go to a comedy club together. If you're feeling especially adventurous, you might also consider attending a seminar or class about improvisational comedy, which are often offered through clubs.

❖ Rent some comedies and spend a weekend having your own private film festival. You might try screening several films with the same star or a variety of comedies from different decades. You might also try movies of live performances of famous stand-up comics.

❖ Know what's funny and what isn't. There shouldn't be too many sacred topics, but if your partner is sensitive about his height, for example, refrain from teasing on that front.

❖ Stock up on humorous cards. After your spouse has had a rough day or a particularly trying week at work, mail him a funny, lighthearted card or leave it on his car dashboard or taped to the front door or bathroom mirror. Remember, too, that you can make your own cards either by hand or on the computer.

FOOD for *Love*

or me, food and romance are forever intertwined. Around the world, throughout recorded history, there have been foods that are believed to inspire passion. While we know now that romance is more in the eye of the beholder than in the effects of a magic elixir, we can still appreciate the allure of special foods. Here are some delectable treats and some ways to enjoy them with your partner. (For Champagne, see "The Romantic Gourmet: Tasting the Stars: Champagne," page 27; for chocolate, see "The Romantic Gourmet: Chocolate—The Divine Indulgence" page 89.)

honey

Honey was the first sweet discovered by humans, and its gooey richness continues to tantalize. An old saying proclaims: "Honey is the dew distilled from the stars and the rainbow." In ancient Babylon, four thousand years ago, a bride's father was supposed to give his new son-in-law all the mead (a beer made of fermented honey)

he could drink for a month; because their calendar was lunar, this time was known as the "honey month," or what is now called the "honeymoon."

Today, "honey" is a term of endearment, and we still treasure the tradition of taking a honeymoon. Think of ways to bring the sweetness of honey into your everyday life. Use honey instead of sugar in your tea, spread honey on toast in place of jam, or chew some honeycomb instead of candy. Have a "honey tasting": Sample several varieties of honey, such as those from different flowers, and decide which you and your partner like best.

At the beautiful Hotel Meurice in Paris, where Bob and I like to stay, I found on a shelf above the hotel room minibar little jars of honey that bear the label Jean Pauctou. I asked the concierge about this, and it turns out that Pauctou is a honey maker who keeps bees on the roof of the Paris Opera House!

pomegranates

Pomegranates are another fruit with strong romantic associations. In ancient Greek mythology, Hades, the god of the underworld, abducted a beautiful woman named Persephone. The young woman was the daughter of Demeter, the fertility goddess. When Demeter appealed to Zeus for help, he told her that her daughter could leave the underworld as long as she had eaten

nothing there. But Persephone had eaten the seed of a pomegranate, and so she was allowed to leave for a while, but had to return to Hades's side for part of each year. Thus pomegranate seeds have become a symbol of an unbreakable tie. Try them to understand why Persephone was so tempted! Toss pomegranate seeds into a salad for a touch of color and sweetness or use some in a spiced compote of winter fruits.

oysters

Oysters have long enjoyed a reputation as a romantic dish, perhaps because Aphrodite, the goddess of love herself, emerged from the ocean on an oyster shell. On a more practical note, the meat of the oyster is rich in minerals, which are believed to boost energy levels and thus stimulate desire. Is it true? Well, the legendary lothario Casanova is said to have eaten oysters raw in the bath every morning. That may be going too far for some, but do try eating them.

Oysters are traditionally eaten raw, served on the half-shell with two or three sauces. Try Worcestershire sauce or an Asian chili sauce, or the classic mignonette, a red wine vinegar sauce with shallots. Because of health concerns with raw seafood, you may wish to cook the oysters before you serve them or order them in an appetizer such as Oysters Rockefeller. Oysters are best eaten during the months ending in r: September, October, November, and December.

strawberries

Strawberries have long been regarded as symbols of love. Red and heart-shaped, they appealed to medieval Europeans as models of perfection. According to some traditions, if a man and woman split a double strawberry, they will fall in love with each other. In France, centuries ago, newlyweds were served strawberry soup because strawberries were regarded as a powerful aphrodisiac. Why not put a strawberry in a glass of Champagne to bring out its flavor? You may already be deeply in love, but there's no harm in following tradition!

caviar

Caviar is actually lightly salted fish roe (eggs). There are many varieties, though only sturgeon roe is considered the real thing. "Caviar" derives from the Persian word "khav-yar" or "cake of strength," as it was thought to have restorative properties and the power to bestow long life. As far back as 2400 B.C., ancient Egyptians began to salt and pickle fish and eggs to store as food for famine and long sea voyages. Perhaps caviar's reputation as a "royal" delicacy dates back to the Middle Ages, when the ruling sovereigns of countries including Russia, China, Denmark, France, and England were given first dibs on any sturgeon that fishermen caught. There are three types of sturgeon that live in the Caspian Sea in Russia, each of which produces roe named after each particular species:

❖ Beluga 000, always referred to as Triple 0 and considered the best and most expensive caviar in the world, comes from the largest and oldest of the sturgeon family, which produce the largest eggs, silvery gray to black and very rich in taste. Beluga needs to mature for at least 25 years before producing its first eggs. The 000 on the label confirms the international standard of exceptional quality for beluga.

❖ Osetra caviar, the second largest sturgeon, produces eggs that are brownish and golden in appearance, with a nutty taste.

❖ Sevruga caviar, the most popular, is grayish in appearance, with a milder, less salty taste.

For a less expensive but delicious caviar, try salmon caviar from Alaska or Canada— large red to orange eggs, lightly salty;

whitefish caviar from Slave Lake, Ontario—small, firm, yellow eggs with a non-fishy, low-salt taste; or paddlefish caviar from the Columbia River in Tennessee and Louisiana—top-quality American caviar, gray to brownish green in color, with a small grain and buttery flavor.

Caviar is delicate and must be served carefully. The one rule to keep in mind is that it must never come into contact with metal. Serve it in a chilled glass bowl with special caviar spoons, which are made of mother-of-pearl or bone (bone spoons are not expensive). Caviar is perfect on its own atop toast points or small warm blini (thin yeast-raised buckwheat pancakes that are a classic Russian accompaniment to caviar) with just a little bit of lemon squeezed over them. I'm a purist and this is the way I like to serve caviar. Some people like to pair caviar with sour cream, minced onion, or chopped hard-boiled eggs. But that's certainly not for me. The onions are too strong and kill the taste of the caviar. And, as far as I'm concerned, eggs are for breakfast!

truffles

Truffles, an exotic type of mushroom found primarily in western Europe, have woven their aphrodisiac spell over the world for four thousand years. In ancient times, everyone from the Babylonians to the Egyptians savored the taste of this delicacy, and truffles were believed to have magical powers. In medieval times, monks were forbidden to eat them lest they be seized by passion. Napoleon had no such qualms; he adored truffles and ate them frequently.

The best-known truffles are the black ones and the white ones. The truffles found in the forests of Périgord, France, have been highly regarded since the fifteenth century. Traditionally hunted with pigs, they are now mainly tracked down by dogs. Today, truffles are very expensive, and they aren't as easily accessible as some of the other romantic foods on this list. Furthermore, the best, most pungent ones are found during only two months of the year, January and February. But truffle oil and sauces are increasingly available, and you'll find that they make a wonderful accompaniment for everything from meat to pasta dishes. But to really experience the subtle delights of a truffle, you might want to visit a fine restaurant and place your palate in the hands of an expert chef.

SECRETS to love: *Trust*

What is the glue that holds a relationship together? It isn't just love. One of the essential ingredients to your happiness together is trust. This is the foundation on which love is built. If trust is absent, it is practically impossible for love to bloom.

Trust means holding a firm belief in the reliability, truthfulness, and courage of another person. It frees you from watching over your partner. He's not a child, and he doesn't need supervision to make sure he's doing the right thing. Your relationship is based on the fact that the two of you have decided to face the world as a team. But when you're apart, which may be frequently because of work or other demands, trust is what lets you keep a light heart and easy mind. Here are some ways I recommend to bring more trust into your life together:

❧ *Trust your partner's word.* If your partner says he will do something, accept that he will and let the subject go. Constant reminders like "You promised to do this…" are not necessary, and they ultimately reveal a lack of trust.

❧ *Trust your partner's decisions.* You may not agree with everything your partner does, but truly having trust in another person requires that you accept the decisions that he makes. You may not agree with how he is handling a crisis at work or a situation with his parents or siblings, for example. While it's your responsibility to talk to him about your concerns regarding a decision he has to make on his own, it's also your responsibility to step back and stop arguing when a decision has been reached. If the outcome doesn't play out as he anticpated, avoid saying, "I told you so."

❖ *Trust your partner's actions.*
I find it very sad that some
people feel the need to spy
on their partners by reading
their regular mail or e-mail
or the papers on their desk
or in their briefcase, or by
going through personal
items. It's a path that will
only lead to doubt down
the road, as there's always
going to be something that
raises questions. If you find
a receipt for flowers he
never gave you, you won't
be able to ask about it and
you won't be able to find
out that they were a going-
away gift for a friend in
his office.

❖ *Trust the future of your
relationship.* It takes a great
deal of trust to overcome
the difficult times and
rough patches that hit
every relationship over the
course of time. But holding
on to the trust between
you lets you ride out the
storms that come your way.
When you emerge from the
clouds, your trust will be
even deeper and your love
immeasurably stronger.

Midnight SNACKS

No matter how much you plan, there will be days
that you and your partner will feel like you hardly see one another. It may be that the only time
you'll get together comes when work is done, the
phone stops ringing, and the kids are in bed.
While you may feel like collapsing yourself, spend
a few moments together enjoying a midnight
snack. Any time after 10:00 P.M. works; you don't
have to wait for midnight. Some suggestions:

▶ Keep the lights turned down. I love dimmer
switches. Burn a scented candle or turn on a light in
the hallway if you're sitting in the kitchen. It makes
for a more romantic setting and the dark has a way
of drawing out secrets.

▶ Speak softly to each other. Even if you aren't afraid
of waking anyone else, there's something alluring
about the sound of a low voice or a whisper against
the hush of the house.

▶ Save talk about the leaky faucet for another time.
This is a chance to focus on each other.

▶ This is a perfect time to plan your fantasy vacation.

▶ Here are some of my favorite easy ideas for
midnight munchies: a small scoop of sorbet with a
cookie or wafer pressed in
the top, a simple sundae
with store-bought caramel
or fudge sauce; cookies
and milk, which brings me
right back to my child-
hood; hot chocolate and
cinnamon toast; a small
tray of cheeses and grapes;
mini-milkshakes served in
glasses with a straw.

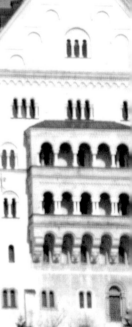

Chapter 5

Romance
around the WORLD
and at home

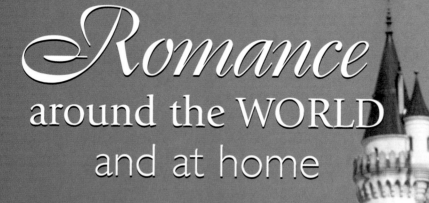

The desire to love and be loved is the one thing we all have in common. Through the centuries, different cultures have fashioned their own traditions and customs to represent and express romantic feelings— have fun adapting some of these ideas for today. Let me take you on your own personal tour of the world of romance.

the international
ART of *Communication*

When we think of communicating with our loved ones, we usually think of having a conversation. But in some cultures around the world, communication is often conducted with signs and symbols rather than spoken words. In the past, this was a necessary device, since unmarried people faced strict rules governing whom they could speak to and what they could talk about. Here are some unusual ways to communicate your feelings:

❖ The Irish have a unique ring called the Claddagh, which communicates the state of one's heart. The ring is made of silver or gold, and it shows two hands holding a heart that is topped with a crown: The hands represent friendship; the heart, love; and the crown, loyalty. Both men and women wear the ring. When it is worn on the right hand by a single person, with the crown pointing toward the heart, it means that heart is free; with the crown pointing away, it means that one is considering love. Or it is worn on the left as a wedding ring. Consider making this tradition part of your own relationship by wearing a Claddagh yourself. They are widely available in North America and are not expensive.

❖ To make a wish with their partners, Bermudians step onto the threshold of a moon gate, a round portal made of stone. This tradition, which originated in ancient China, is so popular that it's not uncommon to find moon gates in people's gardens. Adapt this tradition by choosing a special place where you and your partner can go—perhaps your own garden or a favorite spot in your area— to stargaze and dream aloud together.

❖ In Africa, Zulu maidens have traditionally "written" love letters using beads. The different colors of the beads represent different messages. Red signifies a heart full of love, blue a strong desire to be together, black a feeling of loneliness without one's partner, and white the purity of love. You might fashion a beaded love message to your partner, with a gift tag that interprets the message.

❖ Eleanor of Aquitaine set up her own Court of Love in France in the twelfth century. It was unique in that it was a court ruled by women, and it tried to exert a civilizing influence in all matters, not just in those close to the heart. The court welcomed troubadours, musicians who sang ballads that recounted chivalrous ideals. The troubadours would then travel far and wide, spreading the message of courtly love. Music today still holds strong messages for us. Seek out songs and instrumental recordings that express your feelings for your partner, and share them with him.

A World of *Love* in Flowers

Have you ever heard of "the language of flowers"? This Persian tradition became the craze in Europe in the early eighteenth century, when Lady Mary Wortley Montague, wife of the British ambassador to Constantinople, brought this custom home with her. In Persia, a selam, or bouquet whose symbolic arrangement formed a code, was used to communicate feelings of affection and love. In 1819, a Frenchwoman, writing under the pen name of Madame Charlotte de la Tour, authored Le language des fleurs, *which became a bible for flower symbolism. In Victorian England, middle-class women would spend hours concocting secretly coded bouquets. This wasn't a frivolous pastime; it was actually a way to get around the strict chaperoning and complicated and rigid social rules that governed every aspect of a single woman's life.*

It would be impossible to list all of the meanings of the flowers, since not only did the different flowers have their own meanings, but various hues of the same flower had different messages. For example, red rosebuds told a maiden that she was young and lovely, whereas white rosebuds said that she was too young for love. I do wonder how often messages got crossed this way! But if you want to learn how to send your own secret message to the one you love, buy a book on the subject. Kate Greenaway, the famous author of children's books, also wrote *The Language of Flowers*, which was published in London in 1884 and is still considered a classic. It's currently available in paperback from Dover Publications. You can also type "language of flowers" on a search engine to find Web sites with flower glossaries. Don't forget to write the meaning of your floral message on a card, so that your love will understand what you're telling him! Here are some of the most popular flowers and their meanings:

❧ *Roses*. Roses are among the oldest of cultivated flowers and undeniably the

best-known symbol of love and beauty. An ancient Roman legend explained the beauty of the rose through myths of the gods: Many suitors were lined up to marry a beautiful woman named Rodanthe, but she had little interest in any of them. The men were so full of desire for her that they became rowdy and eventually broke down the doors to her house. This episode angered the goddess Diana, who turned Rodanthe into a flower—the rose— and her suitors into thorns to teach them a lesson. I am partial to white roses, which represent true love, unity, and respect, and pastel roses, such as pink, which represent grace and beauty.

❧ *Daisies*. The daisy as a symbol of innocence harks back to a Celtic legend in which the flowers were believed to come from the spirits of children who  died at birth. To lighten the sad hearts of their parents, God sprinkled daisies all over the earth; hence, their symbolic meaning of innocence and gentleness. English milkmaids placed daisy roots under their pillows to help them dream of love. And traditionally, if you dreamed of daisies in the spring, it was a sign of good fortune to come.

❧ *Pansies*. The pansy represents thoughtfulness, and it was believed to have magical love powers. The Celts made tea from pansies to use as a love  potion. Also, because the petals of a pansy are heart shaped, they were thought to cure a broken heart. One German story tells of how the pansy lost its scent: Once upon a time, pansies had a distinctive, strong fragrance, and people came from miles around just to smell the flower. But by doing this, people destroyed the grass around the pansies, which in turn left no food for grazing cattle. The pansies prayed to the gods for assistance, and their scent was removed, though they were compensated with great beauty.

❧ Here are some other meanings of popular flowers: carnation—admiration, fascination; freesia—innocence; ivy—fidelity, constancy, friendship; jasmine—joy; lavender—devotion, luck, success, happiness; orchid (my favorite flower!)—luxury, refinement, nobility; sweet pea—tender memories; violet—you're in my thoughts.

Romantic GIFTS

The custom of gift giving is an expression of love the world over. Different cultures boast their own gift-giving customs, but the romantic intent rings loud and clear in each instance.

❧ Looking for an unusual present? The lovespoon is a traditional romantic gift in Wales. These intricately carved wooden pieces are decorated with hearts, flowers, or Celtic knots and are for display only. Lovespoons date back to the sixteenth century and they've recently experienced a revival. Antique lovespoons can cost a small fortune at auction, but newly hand-carved ones are lovely and reasonably priced, such as those offered on www.celticlovespoons.com and

www.lovespoons.co.uk, the Web site of The Lovespoon Gallery in Mumbles, Wales.

❧ The tradition of giving a diamond ring for an engagement dates back to 1477, when the Archduke Maximilian of Austria presented one to his intended, Mary of Burgundy. The unique strength of the diamond, one of the hardest substances in nature, symbolized enduring love, and according to one superstition, the diamond was believed to act as a charm that enhanced a man's love for his wife. Diamond rings became popular for royal engagements, but it wasn't until diamond mines were discovered in Africa in 1870 that they became available to a wider population.

❖ Roses have been considered a romantic symbol since ancient times, but they were put to various uses, not just displayed in a vase. The ancient Romans added rose petals to the bath and sprinkled them on the bed and drank rose wine. In Turkey today, jam made from roses is considered a delicacy. Some gourmet food shops sell candied rose petals, and these make a sweet—and unusual—gift for your love. Decorate a homemade cake with them and surprise your partner.

❖ A traditional gift for a nuptial couple in Holland or Switzerland was a pine tree that would be planted outside their home. The tree was believed to represent good fortune. Adapt this custom by planting a tree seedling or another perennial plant with your love. Tend it together, and as it grows, so will your love.

Valentine's day
the world over

The origin of Valentine's Day is full of legend. In the third century A.D., the Roman emperor Claudius II, otherwise known as Claudius the Cruel, was having difficulty rounding up men to serve in his armies. He decided that forbidding marriage would help him recruit soldiers who might otherwise stay with their families. But a young priest named Valentine continued to marry couples and so incurred the wrath of the emperor, who threw Valentine in jail and then had him executed on February 14. While he was incarcerated, Valentine fell in love with the daughter of his jailer. The girl was blind but miraculously had her sight restored before Valentine died. It is said that he wrote a farewell note to her that he signed "From your Valentine."

The celebration of Valentine's Day is patterned after the ancient Roman festival of Lupercalia, which took place on February 15 in honor of Juno, goddess of women and marriage, and Pan, god of nature. Young men and women chose partners for the festival by drawing names randomly from a box. They exchanged gifts and often married. In 496 A.D., Pope Gelasius created St. Valentine's Day to replace the pagan Lupercalia. Here are some ways Valentine's Day has been and continues to be celebrated around the world:

❖ In nineteenth-century Britain, special Valentine buns were baked with raisins, caraway seeds, and plum filling. Find out what your partner's favorite baked treat is, and make it yourself or purchase it from a wonderful bakery. Package the goodies in a decorative box or tin, tie it with ribbon, and leave it on the seat of his car so he sees it early on the morning of Valentine's Day.

❖ The German custom of giving *Freundschaftkartnen*, or friendship cards, became popular in the mid-eighteenth century in England. By the turn of the century, commercial cards had become available. But you can honor the old tradition by making your own Valentine's Day card, just as you did when you were in grade school! Browse in an arts and crafts shop for wonderful papers and decorations to inspire you. Then write your own special message, or use romantic quotations or poetry.

❖ In Italy, unmarried ladies would wake before sunrise on Valentine's Day and watch from their windows for the first man they could see. This would be either the man they would marry or a fellow who resembled him.

❖ In Denmark, a man would send a woman a Valentine *gaekkebrev*, or joking letter, that contained a rhyme and was signed with a series of dots to represent his name. If the lady correctly guessed his identity on February 14, he would reward her with an Easter egg on Easter Sunday that year.

❖ In Japan, Valentine's Day is celebrated with a twist: Women give gifts to men, not the other way around. By giving a present, a woman invokes *giri*, or obligation, which is repaid a month later on March 14 on White Day, when Japanese men give gifts to the women in their lives. Think about following this tradition, especially if a work or personal situation is weighing on his mind around February 14: Buy a gift or cook a special dinner for him, and set a date a month ahead for him to return the favor.

The Incurable Romantic

romantic couples in history

I love a romantic tale, but some of the best are about couples who aren't works of fiction. How much do you know about these well-known duos? Some have sad, even tragic, stories attached to their names, but that makes them linger in our minds perhaps all the more.

▶ *Antony and Cleopatra* (see painting, right). This was the original power couple—Cleopatra the Queen of Egypt and Antony, who was part of the Triumvirate, the group of three men who ruled Rome close to the end of the Republic. But the lovers got too ambitious for their own good, and their plan to conquer Rome was defeated. Instead of surrendering, they decided to kill themselves: Antony by falling on his sword and Cleopatra by letting a poisonous snake, an asp, bite her.

▶ *Queen Elizabeth I and Lord Robert Dudley.* Elizabeth never married because she was sure that she would divide England if she did. Also, she did not want to share her power. As a young girl she had escaped death many times and she knew her power lay with her people. To marry a nonroyal was impossible, and she loved only one man, and all of her life—her childhood friend Robert Dudley. She made him her Master of the Horse and advanced him by making him a peer of the realm—the Earl of Leicester. He was her advisor until his death, and she kept his last letter in a casket by her bed. When she did pass away years later, his name was the last word on her lips.

▶ *Napoleon and Josephine.* Married for thirteen years, this couple had a passionate love affair. Their letters survive today as testimony to their passion. They eventually divorced because Josephine was unable to give her husband what he most wanted: an heir. At their divorce ceremony, each read a statement of devotion to the other. Napoleon's read, in part: "The memory will always remain engraved on my heart." Malmaison, the home that Napoleon and Josephine shared in Paris, is one of my favorite romantic spots to visit. And, by the way, his luck changed the day they divorced—he was never happy again.

▶ *Queen Victoria and Prince Albert.* Royal marriages were arranged by pedigree, and while some of them were companionable, the pairing of Victoria and Albert proved a perfect match. History may have deemed her strait-laced, but Victoria proposed to Albert, and they went on to have nine children. She was devastated by his death in 1861, and though she lived another forty years, she remained in mourning for him until she herself died.

A Wealth
of *Wedding* Lore

Wherever I've traveled in this world, I have found that marriage is cause for celebration—and often a very elaborate one. And whether the budget is large or small, families are devoted to making the day a memory to treasure. Let me share some of what I've learned:

❖ The tradition of wedding rings dates back to ancient Egyptian times. It was an important symbol, with the circle of the ring representing undying love or love with no beginning and no end. But the reason we wear the band on the fourth finger of the left hand is because of the ancient Romans, who believed that a vein ran from that finger directly to the heart.

❖ The kiss that a couple exchanges after they make their vows is romantic, but its origin isn't: The Romans used kisses to finalize legal contracts, as in the term "sealed with a kiss." Honor this tradition by kissing your lover often, even over the smallest "deals" you make, such as agreeing on whose turn it is to do a chore.

❖ White wedding dresses are a modern idea. Anne of Brittany wore one for her marriage to King Louis the XII of France in 1499, but the idea didn't really catch on until the late nineteenth century. In China, brides traditionally wear red, the color of good fortune. Think of wearing white or red when you go out for a special evening, instead of classic "chic" black.

❖ In England in medieval times, guests brought small cakes to the wedding ceremony and the happy couple would kiss over the piled-up cakes. This is the origin of the multi-tiered wedding cake.

❖ An important Hindu tradition is that of *mehndi* (henna)—decorating the bride's hands and feet with intricate and beautiful patterns. It is believed that the darker the *mehndi*, the stronger the love. Applying *mehndi* took hours and was considered an essential pampering ritual. Going to a spa for an afternoon and getting a manicure or pedicure or a makeup lesson will add color, or just indulging in a long, hot bath could be a modern translation of this custom.

the most romantic spot in paris

To me, the whole of Paris is romantic. It's the most beautiful city in the world as far as I'm concerned, and I know it well, having visited it all my life, at least from the age of seventeen. Bob and I lived there for several years while he was running a movie company in Paris. And, incidentally, he grew up in Paris and is practically a native. We try to go back every year, but I cannot single out one spot as the most romantic—I have three, and they're all restaurants. I told you food and romance go hand in hand!

The first is one of our favorite restaurants, Le Tour d'Argent, along the river Seine in the heart of Paris, on the Left Bank. I love this restaurant because of its spectacular view of the Seine, Notre Dame, and the other beautiful buildings in the area. At night, you can look out through the huge plate-glass windows, which pull in views of the river, and see a black velvet sky, jewel-like stars, and the dramatic silhouettes of illuminated buildings—just breathtaking. Inside the restaurant, elegance reigns with antique black glass covering the ceiling, antique pine panelling in between the windows, and lovely candles and flowers throughout. There's no better place for a romantic dinner for two on a special occasion.

Another romantic spot is in the Bois de Bologne, the lovely park on the western edge of Paris. We like to have dinner at Pré Catelan, the *belle époque* restaurant in the middle of the woods.

Last, just outside Paris is a small, cobblestoned town called Barbizon, not far from Fontainebleau (see photo, above), the grand palace and immense park used by the kings of France from the twelfth century. Here is the charming nineteenth-century timbered Hôtellerie du Bas-Bréau, where we recently celebrated Bob's birthday. It was a gorgeous sunny May day, and lunch in the flower-filled garden was superb. We have so many happy memories of Paris, and I believe that remembering the past is romantic, as is returning to places that brought you happiness!

SECRETS to love: *Generosity*

Giving and sharing nurture and celebrate a romantic life. Generosity is defined as a willingness to give, but in romance it's more than that. A willingness to give might be easy to cultivate in a situation of abundance, but a truly generous person is able to give something of herself whatever her circumstances.

❧ *Be generous with time.* The obvious part of this means that you are there for your love when he needs you, or even sensing ahead that he needs time with you. Whenever possible, prioritize the items on your calendar to make time to be together. Make a conscious effort to slow down and shut out the rest of your world once in a while. Also, understand that you both need time apart, too. Be sensitive to your time needs.

❧ *Be generous in how you think and speak.* I think it's a terrible mistake to assume the worst about people. Instead of wasting energy like this, why not think positively about your partner and your relationship, unless there's a proven need to do otherwise?

❧ *Be generous with praise.* People recognize shameless flattery when they hear it, but most people are touched by genuine praise. There's an unfortunate tendency to withhold praise sometimes, for fear of a person developing a swelled head. I think this is nonsense: If you're proud of someone, or if he's done something very well, tell him so. Then tell him again tomorrow. We all need recognition, no matter what our age.

❧ *Be generous in spirit.* The world is not a zero-sum game; another person's gain is not your loss. Cultivate a magnanimous spirit that can be happy and proud of others' successes, and don't feel the need to constantly compare or keep score. Give of yourself freely; the benefits will come back in spades.

Chocolate—
the divine INDULGENCE

Chocolate—culled from the beans of cacao trees—was first discovered centuries ago by the Aztecs, who called it a gift from the gods. The Aztecs served it as a drink, called *xocolatl*, though the taste was not at all like today's hot chocolate. It was very tart and bitter and considered so potent that women were forbidden to drink it!

It was the Spanish explorer Hernán Cortés who brought chocolate to Europe, though it was kept a secret in Spain for the better part of a century. Chocolate had become available throughout Europe by the early seventeenth century, though it took quite a while for *xocolatl* to evolve into what we call chocolate today.

The Europeans changed the recipe, adding sugar or vanilla to give the chocolate a sweeter taste, and men and women alike craved its heavenly flavor. We can thank Daniel Peter, a Swiss chocolate maker, for developing a process for making milk chocolate for eating in 1875; before that, chocolate was sold as cocoa powder or baked into cakes. In 1879, another Swiss, Rodolphe Lindt, invented "conching," the refining process that gave chocolate that melt-in-your-mouth quality.

Here's another piece of chocolate trivia: White chocolate isn't really chocolate at all.

It's a mixture of cocoa butter, milk solids, sugar, vanilla, and sometimes lecithin. (To be real chocolate, it must contain chocolate liquor, the liquid or paste produced from roasted and ground cocoa beans.) It's a lovely treat in its own right, however; European chocolatiers like Valhrona produce a delicious white chocolate. Here are some creative ways to enjoy chocolate:

❱ Try buying a variety of different chocolates for you and your love to sample. Take turns feeding the chocolates to each other.

❱ Fondue is back in style. Melt some chocolate (dark, milk, or white—you pick) in a fondue pot, and dip fresh fruit, such as strawberries or melon and banana slices, into it. Heaven!

❱ Try making your own chocolates. It's easy; you just buy chocolate "drops" (they come in all flavors; you might try marbling dark and white chocolate) and molds at a party or crafts store. Look for heart, angel, or dove molds.

❱ Make a fabulous chocolate dessert to surprise your love. You might try the Heavenly Chocolate Sauce sundae, page 107, or Le Cirque's Chocolate Fondant, page 173.

The Romantic Gourmet

celebrating YOUR
Special days

Everybody loves a celebration, but too many of us save the bells and whistles for the big days like holidays, birthdays, and anniversaries. To live romantically every day, though, don't wait for the big events to reveal your romantic inspirations. This Friday, tomorrow morning, tonight—it's your time to celebrate.

making the most of
your *Weekends*

*I*t's all too easy to zoom through the weekdays and hardly see your partner—you may be living in the same house, but you have little time together because of work, family commitments, and other obligations. While I have to admit that I am sometimes guilty of working through a weekend because of a tough deadline, that has made me value time off all the more. The weekend is your all-important chance to take a breather. Here are some ways to make your weekend special:

❖ Create your own special ritual to mark that the weekend has officially begun. It could be as simple as sharing a cocktail when you've come home from work. (See "The Romantic Gourmet: The Perfect Cocktail Hour for Two," page 103, for ideas.) Or, if you both like to cook, get out all your cookbooks and spend an hour happily leafing through them to devise a menu for Saturday night.

❖ One all-too-common weekend trap is overscheduling: With two ostensibly "free" days, it's easy to get overambitious about what you'll do with your time. Instead, schedule your weekend "together time" first, then build the rest of your plans around that.

❖ Keep a special file labeled "Weekends Only" to hold ideas for activities, day trips, and pastimes you and your partner can do together. Add ideas that inspire you, such as going out to a new restaurant you've read about or going ice-skating, then hold your own special weekend draw. You might decide to go with the first idea you pull out, or you might agree to pull out two and decide together about which one you'll do.

✤ Use the weekend as a time to break some of your rules—or at least bend them a bit! Let the dishes sit in the sink for a little while to allow yourselves the luxury of "wasting time" by simply relaxing together in the backyard and doing

nothing else or reading the newspaper together and doing the crossword puzzle.

✤ Get outside! Too many of us spend so many hours during the week inside: at our desks, in the market, running errands. You might take an impromptu outdoor picnic to a park or scenic spot you've driven by a hundred times and never stopped to enjoy. (See the Provençal Picnic *à Deux*, page 38, and "The Romantic Gourmet: Tips for a Perfect Picnic," page 45, for ideas.)

✤ Take a nap together—and have the fun of waking up together again, but in a more refreshed, relaxed state of mind!

enjoying the
romance of a *Rainy* DAY

Walking in the rain is not everyone's favorite pastime, but I quite enjoy it, provided I have an umbrella and a raincoat! I remember once walking through London with Bob, looking for a cab. We were in Cavendish Square, and as we glanced around, huddled together under our umbrella, I noticed a beautiful sculpture of a mother and child at the end of Deans Mews, which opens off the square. As we went down the mews to take a closer look, I realized that it was the Madonna and Christ, and it was positioned in such a way that it seemed to me she was crying real tears…it was the rain, of course. Later, I found out that this work, by the great English sculptor Sir Jacob Epstein, is called "Madonna and Child." I still believe it was worth getting wet in the rain for! Furthermore, I often go back to look at it when I'm in London.

When we finally managed to get a taxi we headed straight for the Ritz Hotel in Piccadilly, where we had a wonderful English tea—nursery sandwiches, scones with Devonshire clotted cream, strawberry jam, and caraway-seed cake. Afterward, we took another cab to a movie. It was a lovely way to spend a soggy London afternoon. Here are some ideas to make a rainy day romantic:

❖ It can be terribly romantic to forget the umbrella and let yourself get rained on. Think of the ending of the film *Breakfast at Tiffany's*, where the lead characters end up kissing in the rain. There is a great scene at the end of *Hold the Dream*, the miniseries Bob made of my book, where Jenny Seagrove, playing Paula, and Stephen Collins, playing Shane O'Neil, finally get back together—kissing in the rain on the Yorkshire moors.

❖ Treat yourselves to a movie. Bob and I love to do this, and we'll sometimes make a "double feature" out of it. If it's still raining when the movie's over, we buy another ticket and see another film! You might have your own private rainy day film festival. Pick a theme, such as the films of Alfred Hitchcock, one of my all-time favorite directors, or see "The Incurable Romantic: The Ten Most Romantic Movies of All Time," page 165, for a romantic theme.

❖ Use the rain as an excuse not to go outside. Instead, enjoy the luxury of some uninterrupted time together.

✤ If your plans for an outdoor picnic were foiled by the rain, why not have one indoors, or else make a leisurely homemade brunch.

✤ Everyone wishes on stars—why not raindrops? Wait for one that makes an impressive splash against the glass and make your wish. Have your partner do the same.

✤ Watch your wedding video.

✤ There's something so cozily romantic about listening to the raindrops. Sit together in a room where you can hear the pitter-patter on the roof, or curl up together and watch by the windowpane.

✤ Get dressed up and have a cocktail hour—see "The Romantic Gourmet: The Perfect Cocktail Hour for Two," page 103, for ideas. Invite another couple over, if you like.

✤ I love museums and art galleries, and a rainy day is a perfect excuse to go to one. Use this day to see an exhibit together (see the following section for ideas).

A Day at the *Museum*

*A*lthough it's a perfect destination for a rainy day, a museum is a wonderful spot to visit any time with your loved one or to go to alone for romantic inspiration or just to rejuvenate your spirit and your imagination. There's something magical about standing before a piece of art that is centuries old; it lifts you out of your own world, and transports you to a place where time seems unimportant. Museums have a wonderful way of slowing you down and immersing you in another world. And as you walk hand-in-hand through the rooms, you will share the thrill of discovery.

One of my favorite museums in New York City is the Metropolitan Museum of Art. First opened in 1870, it sits on the edge of Central Park. I like it for so many reasons: It's a beautiful space filled with incredible collections, including ancient Greek and Roman art, Egyptian art, European paintings, American decorative arts, and Asian art. So whatever mood I'm in there's always something exciting to see. I also like the fact that I can go there by myself and take in the wonders, and then go back with my husband and see the same rooms with fresh eyes, and get a whole new perspective on what I'm seeing. Here are some ideas for enjoying museums:

❖ Visit your own city or town as if you were a tourist. Read a guidebook to learn about local museums or your local paper to find out about special exhibits that may be going on, and call museums for information.

❖ If paintings aren't your cup of tea, consider these other types of museums: sculpture gardens; rare book exhibits; science museums; museums that focus on every conceivable topic of interest, like historic railways, cars, or dolls; and historic homes and estates that are open to the public. In particular, I love the Arts and Crafts Museum in New York.

❖ If you really enjoy a particular museum, ask if they have courses or seminars available. Many museums offer art instruction classes such as watercolor technique or lecture series on particular periods in art history and individual artists.

❖ Plan a weekend away around visiting a museum you've always wanted to see. But before you book your trip, call the museum to confirm that it will be open; the last thing you want is to find it closed for renovations or to find its collection traveling at the time. Also call the local tourism bureau—most have toll-free numbers; many have Web sites too; you can ask to be sent an information package or at least a brochure to help you plan.

resplendent new england fall foliage

I love the magic of autumn in New England and I enjoy going on long walks through the woods, feasting my eyes on the autumn palette of amber, orange, and crimson leaves. Bob and I used to own a weekend house in Warren, Connecticut, and we still love to visit New England whenever we can.

One of the best ways to enjoy New England foliage is visit the Walden Pond State Reservation in Concord, Massachusetts, where Henry David Thoreau lived in 1845 in his famous cabin, which later became key to the classic work *Walden*. To enjoy fall foliage near water, go to Camden, Maine, where the rich, flaming fall colors are reflected in the waters of Penobscot Bay.

New England boasts wonderful country inns, including my favorite, the Mayflower Inn, in Washington, Connecticut, which makes me feel like I've been transported to the country-side of England or France. Owners Adrianna and Robert Mnuchin were inspired by their fondness for English manors and French *auberges* to open this European-style country house.

Some of the best places to view fall foliage are along highways. Route 100, which runs from one end of Vermont to the other, is particularly picturesque, as is much of Route 7, for example, through Connecticut's Litchfield Hills, where you'll feel as if you've stepped back in time as you cross covered bridges dating back to the Revolutionary War. Here are some ways to capture that special New England fall feeling wherever you live, but if you have the opportunity to travel through New England, call the USDA Forest Service National Fall Color Hotline at 1-800-354-4595 for advice about peak foliage times:

▶ Fall means enjoying evenings by the fire. Add wood chips scented with hickory or applewood to your fire to create a delicious aroma, or find a hotel or inn with a fireplace and watch the crackling flames dance.

▶ To find a scenic drive near you check the National Scenic Byways Web site, www.byways.org.

▶ Spend a day antiquing at an open-air flea market or in a nearby town known for its many antique shops.

Romantic anniversaries, birthdays, and *Holidays*

*E*very day of your life can be romantic, but there are certain days when it's especially *important to focus on romance. Annual events, such as anniversaries and birthdays, deserve extra attention—and affection. So do holidays such as Christmas, which are full of fun for the whole family, but could often benefit from some romantic inspiration. Here's how I like to celebrate standout days on my romantic calendar.*

anniversaries

❖ Bake a small cake for your anniversary dinner. Borrowing from an Italian tradition, put a coin into the cake as you bake it. Tell your partner that whoever finds the coin in their piece of cake gets to make a special request of the other, whether it be for a back rub, breakfast in bed, or another treat.

❖ Instead of just celebrating the day of your anniversary, why not celebrate the whole week? This takes some of the pressure off the one big day and spreads the joy over an extended period of time. Plan your week in advance, with a different "event" each day, whether it be a moonlight walk, a night at the opera, or that skydiving lesson you've been dreaming about.

✤ Write your partner a letter every year to mark your anniversary. Describe what has been special for the two of you in the past year, such as a goal met, an obstacle overcome, a special trip, a memorable day, and remind him of all the reasons you love him.

birthdays

✤ Make your partner's birthday romantic from the start. If his birthday falls on a rushed weekday and there's no time for breakfast in bed, bring a little magic to the table by making him a cup of coffee or tea and setting a note on the saucer telling him the "agenda" for the evening or the coming weekend that he can look forward to all day.

✤ As with an anniversary, a birthday is an important event, so why not spend a week celebrating it? You might not do this every year, but it can be fun for a "big" year, like thirty, forty, or fifty. Spread the joy over a week by doing something special for your love—giving a gift, making a picnic lunch, buying concert tickets—each day that week.

✤ On your birthday, give your partner a romantic surprise by giving him a gift! This is one occasion he definitely won't be expecting it.

new year's eve

✤ Consider staying in on New Year's Eve. Celebrate it as a couple rather than as part of a crowd and create your own romantic evening. You don't have to get dressed up, or you can, if that makes the evening more special. You don't have to drive anywhere, and you don't have to talk to people you don't want to. What a treat!

✤ Make a list of New Year's resolutions together. Figure out what you want to accomplish in the upcoming year as a team. If you have a long-term goal, you might break it down into twelve steps and assign one to each month. Another approach is to make New Year's resolutions that focus on how you want to make more time for romance or improve your relationship. I know of a couple who had split up but wanted to try again. Their first "date" was on New Year's Eve in New York. Throughout a romantic evening that included dinner and a Broadway show, they drafted a set of resolutions to give their relationship a new start. In the early hours of the morning, in the tiny Caffé Reggio in Greenwich Village, the man handed the woman his pen and said, "I have another resolution. Write this down." As he dictated "I promise to love, honor, and cherish you for the rest of my life," he pulled out an engagement ring and proposed to her.

valentine's day

✤ See "Valentine's Day the World Over," page 83, for ideas inspired by customs in different countries.

thanksgiving

✤ Make a list of all of the things you are thankful for in your life. Include your partner at the top, and write out all the reasons you consider yourself lucky to have him.

✤ If you find one year that you're going to be celebrating Thanksgiving with just the two of you, don't feel compelled to dine out, although that can be romantic, too, especially at a country inn that takes you back in time to Colonial America; mark it by cooking together. Try a non-turkey menu, with duck, goose, or your favorite main course.

christmas

✤ Give him one gift tucked under his pillow instead of the tree. It could be a poem you've written for him or another very personal token of your love. Wake him up with a kiss and tell him to look under his pillow.

✤ Celebrate the traditional twelve days of Christmas. Each morning, give your love an envelope with a special message in it. It could contain a clue about a romantic surprise you're planning or a riddle he has to answer before receiving a gift.

✤ Someone I know lost a cherished collection of Christmas ornaments during a move. Inspired by the three gifts the wise men gave to Jesus, my friend's husband gave her three carefully-picked ornaments with a note: "To start our new collection, which we'll gather together and enjoy for years to come." This Christmas, start a new tradition of your very own.

Creating Your
Own *Special* Days

ob and I always celebrate whenever I finish a book. It makes for a wonderful finale, but it also gives me something to look forward to as I sit at my typewriter. We might go to a restaurant or see a

show at the theater. It's especially lovely because I tend to cloister myself in my office as my deadline approaches. This is a wonderful tradition that works for us, but there are many special days a couple might choose to celebrate.

❖ Choose a day as your private anniversary. It could be the day you first met, the day you first kissed, or the day you first said "I love you." Keep this date a secret from everyone else—it's just for the two of you to celebrate.

❖ At the beginning of each month, designate a "Just for Us" day. Block it out on your calendar, and make any arrangements you need to, such as hiring a babysitter,

well in advance. Use the day to do something romantic that you'd never have time for otherwise, such as enjoying a special outing or dancing the night away.

❖ Celebrate your half-birthdays. This is an especially good idea if your or your partner's birthday falls around a traditional holiday time. If his birthday is December 25, celebrate his half-birthday on June 25. Do cake, candles, and gift—the whole nine yards.

❖ Pick a certain day of the month to celebrate. It could be the date of your anniversary, or it could just be the second Saturday of every month. Then take turns planning ways to celebrate that day. Use it as an opportunity to surprise each other.

❖ Who says Friday the 13th has to be an unlucky day? Make it your own special tradition to celebrate it whenever it rolls around. You might do a dinner at a favorite restaurant, or go for a walk by moonlight.

The Incurable Romantic

rainbows

One of the reasons I love rainy days is that I look forward to seeing a rainbow when the rain ends and the sun breaks through. Below is a painting by one of my favorite artists J. M. W. Turner. Rainbows are beautiful in their own right, but they are also the stuff of myth. They have traditionally been viewed as a bridge between heaven and earth, and that's how I like to think of them. Here are some ways to enjoy rainbows—come rain or shine:

▶ Read a book of mythology that contains rainbow lore. Many Native American tribes

have rainbow stories: For example, in one Anishnabe myth, it is the Daughter of Rainbows who gives the butterfly its colors. Read aloud to your partner on a rainy day, or write out a myth on paper decorated with rainbow hues and give it to your love.

▶ The rainbow is traditionally a symbol of promise—it marks the end of the Great Flood in the Book of Genesis. When you see a rainbow, make a renewed pledge of love to your partner.

▶ There's no one best place to view a rainbow, but both a flat landscape or an elevated viewing spot, such as the top of a building or a hill, will let you see more of the rainbow.

▶ Wearing sunglasses actually makes the rainbow easier to see.

▶ Hang up a crystal prism or stained-glass rainbow in your window to enjoy the rainbow effect on any sunny day.

SECRETS to Love:
Loyalty

*L*oyalty may be an old-fashioned idea, but its relevance to your relationship is as strong as it ever was. In its deepest sense, loyalty means being faithful, steadfast, and devoted in your love. It's part of what cements your relationship, and it's part of what puts your relationship above all others. Here are some ways loyalty can come into play in your relationship:

❧ *Be loyal to your partner in front of others.* If you hear unfair criticism of him, or are told a joke at his expense, such as when family members may carry teasing too far, don't be shy about expressing your disapproval. Never say anything critical about your partner in public.

❧ *Be loyal to your partner's secrets.* Whatever he tells you in confidence stays in confidence. There are no exceptions to this rule, not even your mother or your best friend.

❧ *Be loyal to your relationship.* Loyalty to your partner means putting your relationship ahead of all others.

Your relationships with family (and probably some of your close friends) predate your partner, but your first allegiance is to the person you've chosen to share your life with.

❧ *Be loyal to your partner in tough times.* Don't give up on your partner or his dreams because you've had a setback. All relationships have their ups and downs. Loyalty is especially important during the difficult moments, and your support is essential to getting things back on track.

The Perfect Cocktail Hour
for TWO

When the two of you are done on your busy workdays, having your own private cocktail hour is a wonderful way to reconnect. While I'm not much of a drinker, I do enjoy the Champagne cocktail, Kir Royale. Bob will sometimes have a vodka cocktail, which we make with Ketel One, a Dutch vodka that it best served ice-cold. Here are some ways to enjoy your own private cocktail hour:

◗ Set the scene by dimming the lights and putting on some music. I am a Frank Sinatra fan, and a cocktail hour is a wonderful time to listen to his romantic songs.

◗ Buy a book that contains recipes for different cocktails and try making them together. You may discover some new favorites. Or if you really want to experiment, try making up your own special cocktail.

◗ Make up your cocktails using a classic shaker. Other traditional bar accoutrements include silver-tone barware such as decorative swizzle sticks, ice tongs, ice bucket, cocktail strainer, jigger, bottle opener, and martini sticks for olives.

◗ My father said that a drink always tastes better in a nice glass, and I still believe this. Have a special set of glasses that you use only for your cocktail hour together. Educate yourself about highball glasses, martini glasses, margarita glasses, and the like.

◗ Have a toast before you drink as part of the ritual: Toast each other, your future together, or make up something romantic on the spot.

◗ Try different drinks to fit the season. Summer is a great time for a margarita or a mint julep, while winter is a perfect time for a hot toddy or Irish coffee.

◗ Have some nibbles on hand to enjoy with your drinks, such as a cheese board. (See "The Romantic Gourmet: French Cheese Primer," page 138, for ideas.)

◗ If you don't drink alcohol, you can still enjoy a cocktail hour with an imported sparkling water, seltzer, or exotic fruit juice. Just add a twist of lime or lemon—and don't forget to toast.

intimate celebratory dinner

In my novel, A Woman of Substance, *Emma arranges for the catering department at Harte's to prepare an engagement dinner for one hundred guests to celebrate the upcoming nuptials of her brother Frank and his fiancé, Natalie. I've adapted this menu for a romantic dinner for you and your intended or to celebrate any special occasion: a birthday, anniversary, promotion, or even just rejoice in your love for each other on an "ordinary" day.*

The menu begins with a classic roast chicken—the epitome of a home-cooked meal and a symbol of love and caring—and ends with a divine ice cream sundae. To make the first course, Smoked Salmon with Whole Wheat Bread and Butter, soften some butter and pack in a ramekin. Serve alongside sliced whole grain bread, cut diagonally in half, and smoked salmon ruffled on a serving plate or on two individual plates. Easy and gorgeous. Here are some ideas to make your celebration unforgettable:

— *Menu* —

Smoked Salmon with Whole Wheat Bread and Butter (see above)

Lemon Roast Chicken with Potatoes, Shallots, and Garlic

Fresh Green Beans with Lemon Parsley

Heavenly Chocolate Sauce over Vanilla Bean Ice Cream Garnished with a Tête-à-Tête of Mixed Fresh Berries

❖ If the dinner is in honor of your upcoming marriage, invite your fiancé to dinner at your home. When he arrives, give him a special engagement present. If the dinner has a different theme or purpose, present your partner with a small gift that reflects what you love most about him. It need not be store-bought, but rather should express your feelings, such as a love letter. To learn more about the art of the perfect love letter, see "The Incurable Romantic: Love Letters," page 50.

❖ To add a romantic, sweet touch to your table setting, place a folded napkin on each dinner plate, with the flatware on top, and tie with pink satin ribbon and add a sprig of baby's breath. Or group three cream-colored pillar candles of different heights, each encircled by a small ring fashioned from fresh baby pink rosebuds (ask your florist to help you).

❖ Before dinner, toast your love with Champagne. To brush up on your know-how, see "The Romantic Gourmet: Tasting the Stars: Champagne," page 27.

❖ Let music add to the intimacy of the setting. One of my favorite classical composers is Mozart. For dinner music, try his piano quintets, such as the Quintet for Piano and Woodwinds, K. 452.

Lemon Roast Chicken with Potatoes, Shallots, and Garlic

If you want flavor to really permeate the chicken, the best way is to tuck the flavoring ingredients under the skin before roasting. It's easy: Just use your fingertips to gently separate the skin from the breast meat, add the ingredients (in this case lemon butter), and smooth with your hands to spread it evenly. For myself, I leave the garlic out of this recipe, but I know many people are partial to the flavor, so it's optional.

3 tablespoons unsalted butter,
  at room temperature
2 teaspoons finely grated lemon zest
Salt and freshly ground pepper
One 3-pound chicken, patted dry
1 lemon, cut into 8 wedges
8 baby red potatoes, scrubbed
4 small shallots, peeled
4 garlic cloves, unpeeled

1. Preheat the oven to 400°F.
2. Stir together the butter, lemon zest, $^1/_4$ teaspoon salt, and $^1/_4$ teaspoon pepper

in a small bowl. Place the butter mixture under the skin of the chicken breast and spread evenly. Tuck the wing tips under the chicken. Place the lemon wedges in the chicken cavity and tie the legs together. Place the chicken on a rack in a large roasting pan and add the potatoes, shallots, and garlic to the pan. Season the chicken, potatoes, shallots, and garlic with $^1/_2$ teaspoon salt and $^1/_4$ teaspoon pepper.
3. Roast the chicken for 1 hour and 15 minutes, or until the thigh juices run clear when pierced with a small paring knife,

basting the chicken with the juices and tossing the potatoes, shallots, and garlic every 10 to 15 minutes.

4. Place the chicken on a cutting board and let stand 10 minutes to set the juices for easier carving. Carve the chicken and arrange on serving plates along with the potatoes, shallots, and garlic.

Serves 2 with leftovers.

Fresh Green Beans with Lemon Parsley

The clean, fresh flavor of the parsley really enhances the beans. If you happen to have some slivered mint, it would add a lovely dimension, also.

2 cups trimmed and halved fresh slender green beans (from about 8 ounces)
I tablespoon olive oil
I tablespoon chopped fresh parsley
1/2 teaspoon finely grated lemon zest
1/4 teaspoon salt
A pinch of freshly ground pepper

1. Bring a medium saucepan (about three-quarters) full of salted water to a boil over high heat. Add the green beans and cook for 3 to 5 minutes, until bright green and crisp-tender. Drain in a colander; refresh under cold running water to stop the cooking and drain on paper towels. If not using immediately, wrap in damp paper towels and store in a plastic bag in the refrigerator for up to 1 day.

2. To serve, heat the olive oil in a medium skillet over medium heat. Add the green beans, parsley, lemon zest, salt, and pepper and cook, stirring, for 1 to 2 minutes, until heated through.

Serves 2.

c o u n t d o w n   t o   s u c c e s s

I Day Ahead
➡ Prepare the lemon butter for the Lemon Roast Chicken
➡ Trim, halve, and blanch the green beans
➡ Make the Heavenly Chocolate Sauce

I Hour Ahead
➡ Whip the heavy cream and store, tightly covered, in the refrigerator

➡ Soften the butter for the Smoked Salmon with Whole Grain Bread

15-30 Minutes Ahead
➡ Take the ice cream out of the freezer just to soften slightly
➡ Arrange smoked salmon on plate(s) and cover with plastic wrap

Heavenly Chocolate Sauce over Vanilla Bean Ice Cream Garnished with a Tête-à-Tête of Mixed Fresh Berries

Although no one knows for certain the derivation of the word "sundae," some credit it to the owner of a Midwestern soda fountain in the 1800s. As the story goes, at that time, the favorite ice cream delight was an ice cream soda, but blue laws prohibited the consumption of carbonated beverages on Sunday. So, the soda fountain clerk topped ice cream with a syrup to create a "dry" soda called a sundae, so as not to be sacrilegious. There's nothing like a fudgy, not too sweet, warm chocolate sauce over ice cream, and ripe fresh berries make it irresistible. Try a combination of sliced strawberries, blueberries, raspberries, and blackberries—or your favorite mix. Add a dollop or two of whipped cream, if you're feeling extravagant. Use real whipped cream in the can, if you'd rather not whip your own.

1/4 cup heavy cream

I teaspoon sugar

1/4 teaspoon pure vanilla extract

I pint good-quality store-bought all-natural
   vanilla ice cream (or your favorite flavor)

Heavenly Chocolate Sauce, warmed
   (recipe follows)

1/4 cup mixed fresh berries

1. Whip the cream with the sugar and vanilla in a small bowl with a whisk or hand-held mixer just to soft peaks. Can be made up to 1 hour ahead.
2. Place 2 large scoops of ice cream into each sundae dish or bowl. Pour the chocolate sauce over each serving, sprinkle with the berries, and top with the whipped cream. Serve immediately.

Serves 2.

Heavenly Chocolate Sauce

1/4 cup water

5 tablespoons sugar

1/4 cup unsweetened cocoa powder

3 tablespoons heavy cream

Bring the water and sugar to a boil in a small saucepan over high heat, stirring until the sugar is dissolved. Remove the pan from the heat and whisk in the cocoa powder and cream. Return the pan to medium-low heat and cook, whisking, about 2 minutes, or just until thickened slightly. Can be made up to 1 day ahead. Store at room temperature, then gently reheat to serve.

Chapter 7

Romantic SURPRISES

Variety is the spice of life—and love. We know the importance of having a good routine, but breaking out of that structure is half the fun—and it can jump-start romance. Be bold. Take some chances. Do something that you've never done before. Be open to the possibilities around you, and if you don't see them, make your own. Remember, everyone loves surprises.

the *Power* of the Unexpected

While I enjoy the comfort and predictability of the habits and routines Bob and I have settled into over the course of our marriage, we both know it's important to leave room for the unexpected. Bob's favorite gift from me was a painting of our beloved dog Gemmy, a bichon frise. I had seen the work of Christine Merrill, America's foremost painter of animals, at the William Secord Gallery in New York, and I commissioned her to paint Gemmy's portrait—without telling Bob.

Before the picture was finished, Gemmy suffered an embolism during an operation on her knee, and sadly she died. To mark Gemmy's passing, Christine added two small teardrops on the leaves of a flowering plant in the bottom right-hand corner. When I presented the picture to Bob, he was overwhelmed. It is so lifelike that he felt Gemmy was about to step out of the frame. The picture now hangs in our bedroom.

There are many ways you can make room for the unexpected in your life together:

❖ Plan a getaway weekend for the two of you. Let him know in advance when you're going so that he doesn't make other plans, but don't tell him anything else. Then whisk him away to a country inn or other special destination.

❖ Buy him a gift that he's wanted for ages but has refused to get because he doesn't want to spend the money on himself. Or buy him a gift that he doesn't even realize he wants, like the portrait of Gemmy I gave to Bob.

❖ Transform one room in your house or your backyard or patio into a romantic destination. For example, invite your love to join you at a "Parisian café" and serve up croissants and cheeses or "tea on the lawn" and wear all white.

❖ Get him something that relates to one of his interests or passions, something that you normally don't show an interest in. It could be tickets to a game or an autograph from one of his heroes or movie stars whom he's always wanted to meet. Don't wait for his birthday to give it to him—

tape the tickets to the bathroom mirror on a Monday morning.

❖ Host a surprise birthday party for him. You may want to let him know that his family will be dropping by so that he isn't caught completely unaware, something that makes some people uncomfortable, but keep the lengthy list of friends a secret.

❖ Sometimes Bob just calls me and says, "Meet me at the Barrymore Theater," or he might just give an address and a time, then he surprises me with tickets to a play or to the ballet. Telephone your partner late in the day and give him an address and time to meet you. Don't tell him that you've made a reservation at a restaurant he's never been to before—keep him guessing.

creating little *Surprises* for your partner

Big plans are grand, but I think that little surprises are key to living romantically every day. Sometimes, it's not only what you do but how you do it. For example, while Bob was traveling on business in London, he went to my favorite boutique and bought me a beautiful cream silk coat. He had it delivered directly to me in New York by overnight courier, with a romantic note. He likes to bring me gifts when he's been away, but the way he presented this gift made it a real surprise!

If you choose to make your surprise a gift (there are lots of nongift ideas below), put a lot of thought into what you will buy—yes, it's the thought that counts, not the price. Put your energy into thinking of something that would really please or surprise him and that relates to a strong interest or

passion. For example, Bob knows I love historical biographies, and on one recent trip to London, he bought me Antonia Fraser's biography of Marie Antoinette as well as another important biography on the Brontë sisters, among my favorite writers from my native Yorkshire. Here are some little surprises you might try. And remember, they need not be extravagant:

❖ For dessert, get a cake that has a favorite photograph of the two of you "printed" on the top; many bakeries offer this service.

❖ Make an appointment for him to have a professional massage without telling him. Just send him out with the correct address and instructions to give his name at the desk. Arrange in advance to pay for the treatment, including the tip.

❖ Once, I asked our cook to make a dinner of all Bob's favorite foods,

including his ultimate favorite, lamb stew. He thanked me so sweetly later in the evening, even though I hadn't actually cooked it! Secretly ask your spouse's mother for the recipes for or just the names of all of his favorite dishes from his childhood. Then, for a romantic surprise one night, serve them up, one after another, from appetizer to main course to dessert.

❖ Send a personalized gift basket to him at the office, filled with all of his favorite treats or with frivolous items, like bubble gum or the latest issue of a favorite magazine. Sign it "From your not-so-secret admirer." Or leave it at the foot of the bed or on his desk in his home office.

❖ Get a photograph of your love as a child from his parents or a relative. Put it in a double frame with a picture of you as a child, and leave it on his bedside table.

❖ Without telling him in advance, arrange for the kids to be away at a relative's or the babysitter's for an evening. Savor the time to yourselves.

the most romantic spot in london

As far as I'm concerned there is more than one romantic spot in London, and any number of romantic things to do with the one you love. My husband Bob loves boats, yachts, ships, almost anything that sails, in fact; and I once invited him for dinner on a boat on the Thames, one of the world's most famous rivers. I recommend taking one of the luxury boats, such as the *Symphony*, that board on the Embankment near Cleopatra's Needle, the famous monument. As the boat sails off into the moonlight, cocktails and a multiple-course gourmet dinner are served onboard. It's lovely to drink and eat as the boat sails down the river, and you get a wonderful view of London in all its glory, including the houses of Parliament, Big Ben, the London Eye, the Tower Bridge, the Tower of London, the Millennium Dome, and more.

Royal monarchs, on their elaborate barges, often used the river as a fast way to get from castle to castle, and they too ate and drank and caroused on their barges! I also think of the dinner boats as England's answer to the *bateau mouches* that float along the River Seine in Paris. The London boats go all the way to the Thames basin and back.

If you are celebrating a special event, such as a birthday or a wedding anniversary, and don't mind a big tab, you can dine at the Waterside Inn in the sixteenth-century village of Bray on the banks of the Thames. I think it's one of the most beautiful and romantic inns. It is owned by the famous Roux brothers, who also own the renowned Gavroche restaurant in London. The food is out of this world, and, of course, the gardens and the river views are spectacular, especially in the summer months, when you can take an aperitif or coffee in one of the two summerhouses on the terrace overlooking the river and watch the swans and riverboats glide by.

the *Spirit* of adventure

I don't particularly like jaded people who think they've been everywhere and seen and done everything already. That attitude is a killjoy for romance. Life is an adventure to be savored. I've had the opportunity to travel, meet a lot of people, and do many interesting things, and I feel profoundly fortunate. My motto could be: "Been there, done that—and still doing it!" Welcome the spirit of adventure into your life. Here are some thoughts to get you started:

❖ Try a sport that requires you to have absolute trust in your partner, such as rock climbing or scuba diving. You don't need to go into the great outdoors for this: a climbing gym will give you a taste of what it's like.

❖ Plan a vacation in a country where the national language isn't one you know. You may need to plan this a couple of years in advance if this is a big-ticket item, but it's worth it! Trust each other and your guidebook as you explore this unfamiliar territory. If you're planning well in advance, take a language course together to help you prepare.

❖ Play a game that involves asking your partner different questions about his opinions and beliefs. You may learn things about him that you never expected and vice versa.

❖ Make a list together of all the places you'd like to go and things you'd like to do. Let yourself dream. If you've always

❖ Have dinner at a restaurant with an ethnic cuisine you've never tried. Take turns choosing a place to go.

❖ Hop on a roller coaster together. Feel free to cling to each other—and scream—at the twists and turns.

❖ Paint a room in your home a bold or unusual color. My dining room is a warm, bright raspberry red, which I love, but it might not be for everyone. Think about what you'd like. If you tire of the color after a while, it's easy enough to paint it again.

❖ You're never too old to go sleigh-riding or sledding. All that's required is snow!

❖ Attend a concert of music you may not be very familiar with, like jazz or choral. Keep an open mind and listen with your heart. You might just find you like it!

wanted to go to the moon, write it down! Then think of how you can make some of these dreams come true. For example, we can't all be astronauts, but we can visit a planetarium or make a pilgrimage to Cape Canaveral.

enriching your *Relationship*

An integral part of living romantically every day is growing and expanding your relationship. Keep abreast of what's going on around you. I like to do it by reading—our apartment is full of American news magazines, British magazines and newspapers, and books—and I like to watch the news on television in the evenings as well. My husband

and I share a passion for discussing current events. This isn't everyone's cup of tea, so what you need to do is to decide what you're interested in learning about. Here are some ideas:

❖ Take a wine-tasting class together. Learning about wine is a serious business, but it's a lot more fun when you get to sample different varieties. (See "The Romantic Gourmet: A Beginner's Wine Primer," page 120, to get you started.)

❖ Go to a reading by a writer who one or both of you admire. Local bookstores and universities often arrange these events, and the fee is minimal or free. Or else go to a reading by an author you're not familiar with. A wonderful series in New York is "Selected Shorts" at Symphony Space on the upper West Side, where famous actors read short stories; it also airs on National Public Radio.

❖ Spend an afternoon in a ceramics workshop open to the public. Working with clay can be incredibly sensual.

❖ Sign up for a cooking lesson with a chef. This can be done through a cooking school or an adult education course. Some restaurants also host their own classes.

❖ Start your own "book club" just for the two of you. Agree to read the same book, then discuss it. You don't have to wait till you get to the end.

❖ There's nothing more romantic than taking a dance class together. You can sign up for lessons at many gyms as well as dance schools; a less formal option is to go early to a nightclub when they offer instruction while the night is still young. Ballroom dancing is a traditional favorite, and Latin dance is famously romantic.

❖ Learn a new sport together. You might try taking tennis or golf lessons, or anything you're curious about. Don't put it off.

❖ Attend a lecture on a hot topic in current events. Experts speak at universities, colleges, and pubic libraries, or are hosted by local political or social organizations. Get on some mailing lists and avidly read the calendar section of your local paper.

Long Distance
Romance

ob and I have never officially had a long-distance romance, but we've experienced the symptoms of it up close. Bob travels frequently on business, and when I'm not at home writing, I sometimes need to travel to promote my books. This has put us in different time zones and kept us out of each other's company for longer than we'd like. I know also that the reality today is that many couples spend a great deal of time apart, usually because of the demands of work or school. The world may be getting smaller, but that makes long-distance love no less challenging. Here are some ways to cope:

❧ Keep in contact every single day. Communication is key to sustaining a long-distance romance. There is nothing that can replace the intimacy of talking each day, even if it's for just a few minutes. The ideal time to talk is before bedtime, so that your love's voice is the last thing you hear that day. But if this isn't possible because you're in different time zones, keep in mind that what's essential is to share the details of your day. "Catching up" with a phone call spaced more than

a few days apart becomes increasingly harder the more time goes by.

❧ Use technology. E-mail is a wonderful, and inexpensive, way to tell him about something that has just happened, to forward an article you find interesting, or just to say that you love and miss him.

❧ Make a tape for your partner so he can hear your voice whenever he wants to. You can think of it like a radio show:

Speak for a bit, then play a song that holds memories for the two of you. You might also want to read a poem you've composed yourself (or see "The Incurable Romantic: Love Poems," page 66, for ideas) or a passage from a book.

❧ Send cards and letters, and be fearlessly romantic in them. When you're far away, your love will have these mementos to hold onto, to treasure with each re-reading.

❧ Make your own "wallpaper" (background screen) for your computer, a great way to be reminded of how much you love your partner. Use a photo, such as a favorite vacation spot you visited together, or a candid shot of the two of you.

❧ Set up long-distance "dates." Pick a day or weekend and agree to see a certain movie at the theater or on video. Then you can share the experience by discussing it afterwards. A variation is to both agree to read a particular book within a given timeframe, say, a month; this is a little trickier to coordinate, but it's another way to share experiences without actually being together.

❧ Send a care package. If your love's favorite chocolate-chip cookies come from your local bakery, put some into an airtight container and ship them overnight. If you like, get creative and make a themed care package, such as an "international basket" with packaged gourmet foods from different countries or a "downtime basket" with a novel by a favorite author, a bookmark, warm socks, and snacks. A classically romantic idea is to send your lover a lock of your hair (save some from your next haircut). Tie it with some ribbon so that there are no stray strands.

❧ It's very romantic to leave a small article of your clothing, such as a scarf or a casual weekend shirt, with your partner. Dab some of your perfume on it; smelling the familiar scent will unleash a host of memories.

While we might dream of getting away from it all, our responsibilities usually keep us tied to home. Fortunately, some of the most romantic places you can go together aren't far away. When we're in London, Bob and I will wander through the beautiful grounds of Kensington Gardens. We are still in the city, but we emerge refreshed and recharged. Here are some other ways to get away, even if you can't go too far:

▶ Clip articles from the newspaper about interesting sites in your area, special festivals, house tours, and so forth. Keep them in a file and choose a spot together when you're ready to go.

▶ Sign up for an aerial tour by hot-air balloon. This will give you a wonderful new perspective on your town or city.

▶ Spend a day at the zoo— without the kids in tow.

▶ Enjoy a walk through a botanical garden. Some of these preserves have different features, such as a labyrinth, exotic hothouse, bird sanctuary, or rose garden, that you might find particularly interesting. If you don't have one in your immediate area, research to see if the closest city near you has one; many,

like Boston, have public gardens, which can be lovely, too.

▶ Take an extended hike in the woods. Bring a picnic lunch with you to enjoy; afterward, you might want to have dinner at a rustic inn or restaurant.

▶ Spend a day on the water, perhaps taking a tour by boat or kayaking, if you're more adventurous.

▶ Rummage through antique shops or visit country auctions or flea markets for a day. You don't need to buy anything; the fun is in the looking. If you find a real gem together, consider it an added bonus.

▶ Take a train to another town for a local festival or theater production, or just to happily explore its unfamiliar streets at a leisurely pace.

SECRETS to Love: *Kindness*

*I*mages of passion are what come to mind initially when we think of romance. But there is a gentler side too, which can be called kindness. Somehow we associate this quality with how we should treat those who are

vulnerable, such as young children or the elderly. But there is a vulnerable side to every person, and kindness is key to fostering love.

What is kindness exactly?

It's a tender regard for another person's well-being, a gentle expression of regard that is at the root of true friendship. It's part of wanting what's best for the one you love and treating him with care. It requires a generous mind-set, an ability to look beyond our own wants and desires and consider what would make others happy. Here are some ways to put kindness to work in your relationship:

❧ *Be kind in small ways.* Think of your partner when you make even the smallest decisions, even if it's about what to have for dinner. Kindness is in the details, like remembering to call him after he's had a doctor's appointment or running an errand

that he can't fit into his schedule. Think about what would make life easier and more enjoyable for your partner and do it.

❧ *Be kind every day.* Kindness is a habit that we need to grow into. It's very natural to think first about what we want; it takes maturity to consider others. But if you practice kindness each and every day, you will reap the benefits in your relationship.

❧ *Be kind to the world outside your door.* Those who are truly kind don't forget about kindness when they are away from home. Think of how we cringe when we see someone speaking rudely to a clerk in a shop or a waiter at a restaurant. Kindness is something we need to carry with us everywhere.

❖ *Be kind to yourself.* Sometimes even very kind people act like bullies, but only toward themselves. They berate themselves for every little thing that goes wrong or doesn't turn out exactly according to plan. Let go of your unfair expectations and let yourself relax. Don't ever forget that you deserve love and kindness too. Being kind to yourself helps you be kind to others.

A Beginner's WINE primer

Learning about wine is one of the great pleasures in life. While we might not be oenophiles, that's the technical word for a wine connoisseur, who can nail down a wine's vintage with a mere sniff, learning about wine is a wonderful way to enrich your relationship. Here are ten of the most popular types of wines:

Reds

❱ Cabernet sauvignon. Often referred to as the "King of Red Grapes," this is a medium- to full-bodied, densely colored red wine, often with a rich berry flavor. The grape originated in the Medoc region of France. It is a very complex wine that also blends well with other grapes; for instance, a cabernet merlot has a softer, more subtle finish than a pure cabernet. California, Australia, and Chile also produce fabulous cabernet sauvignons.

❱ Merlot. This popular cousin of cabernet sauvignon is very rich and complex, but it's a bit mellower in taste and may contain scents of plums, black cherry, toffee, chocolate, violets, orange, and tea. Many California wineries produce outstanding merlots, which don't need the careful attention to aging that cabernets do.

❱ Pinot noir. This red wine, often ruby in color, is at once rich and delicate, elaborate but accessible. Many can be drunk at a young age, but even with aging, they keep their graceful nature. While there are some excellent French pinot noirs, also try those from California and Oregon, where the pinot noir grape grows well (and those domestic bottles are often less pricey).

❱ Syrah. Hailing from the Rhone valley in France, this grape produces a strong, full-bodied red wine, sometimes called "the manliest of all wines" because of its meaty, smoky overtones. When young, French syrah is sometimes spicy or fruity; as it ages, more complex layers of spice, violets, rose petals, blackberries, or black pepper emerge. The grape is called "shiraz" in Australia.

◗ Gamay. This is the grape that produces French Beaujolais, a wine meant to be drunk young. Unlike many red wines, this is one that is quite fruity and light.

◗ Zinfandel. Wine experts disagree about this "mystery" grape; its exact European origins are not known. According to some experts, the first California bottled zinfandels appeared as early as 1883. Red zinfandel wines are dry, full-bodied, intense, and even peppery. White zinfandel is blush-colored, light, fruity, sweet, and best served chilled. This popular wine is made by separating the white juice from dark grape skins before any hint of color can seep into the juice.

Whites

◗ Chardonnay. Popular the world over, this dry white wine comes from the green-skinned European vinifera grape. In France, the chardonnay grape is used to create the great white Burgundy wines, among which Pouilly-Fuisse is one of the most popular. North America also produces excellent chardonnays. Chardonnay wine can embrace many different flavors and nuances: Depending on the ripeness of the grape, you may

sense hints of green apple, citrus, figs, pineapples, ripe apples, melons, and honey. Most chardonnays are aged in oak barrels, imparting an oaky, vanilla, caramel, or buttery flavor.

◗ Pinot gris (rhymes with GREE). This grape makes a rich, silky-smooth, dry, full-bodied white wine. Popular in Europe, especially in Alsace and Italy, it is called "pinot grigio." The best pinot gris wines in the United States are are said to come from Oregon.

◗ Riesling. This grape, grown traditionally in Germany and Alsace but also in Washington state and Oregon, produces a fragrant wine with a fruity or floral bouquet that can range from very dry to surprisingly sweet dessert wines. California Rieslings tend to be delicate, with a hint of melon; German Reislings may be slightly tart with a hint of grapefruit.

◗ Sauvignon blanc. This crisp, dry white wine, which has hints of olive, herb, and smokiness, inspired California vintner Robert Mondavi to rename it fumé blanc (smoky white) in the 1960s, in one of the smoothest marketing moves in wine history. A French classic from the Loire valley, lovely sauvignon blancs also come from all over the world, including California, South Africa, and New Zealand. The grape was introduced to the United States in 1878, when the Marquis de Lur Saluces gave some cuttings of the grape from the renowned Château d'Yquem to winemakers Louis Mel and Charles Wetmore in Livermore, California.

Chapter 8

Love and AFFECTION

There are many ways to express romantic feelings, including hugs and kisses. Humans respond to touch instinctively. Affection can be shown in a variety of ways—wrap your partner in the embrace of your love. Fill each day of your life with love—starting right now.

the *Romance* of the KISS

The kiss is perhaps the greatest symbol of romance. Kisses have provided some important turning points in my books, and they've been just as important to me in my own life! A wealth of legends surrounds kissing. Here are some particularly fascinating ones, plus some ideas about how to incorporate more kisses into your own romantic life:

❖ In ancient Rome, kisses were taken as seriously as an oath. It actually became law that if a man kissed a virgin in public, she had the right to press for his hand in marriage.

❖ Kissing under mistletoe is an ancient Celtic custom. The plant was believed to have magical powers, including the ability to bestow fertility upon a couple.

❖ In Europe, kissing on both cheeks is customary when you meet a friend or sometimes even an acquaintance. This custom evolved from a feudal tradition in observance of which lords and ladies of equal stature kissed each other upon both cheeks as a greeting.

❖ During the Medieval Age of Chivalry, being a good kisser was considered an essential quality for a knight.

❖ Kissing the famous Blarney Stone in County Cork, Ireland, is said to bestow the gift of eloquence.

❖ While they're not written on your calendar, let kisses punctuate your day, starting when you say good-bye to your partner on your way to work in the morning and resuming later in the day when you reconnect.

❖ The act of kissing has served as an inspiration to many artists. Perhaps the most famous is Auguste Rodin's "The Kiss," which he sculpted in marble in 1886 and is now housed at the Rodin Museum in Paris.

❖ Develop your own kissing "repertoire," from a short peck to a lingering embrace, and use it everyday.

❖ Sneak out of a party together and share a few moments to kiss. This will feel illicit—even though it's not!

❖ Send your partner a card or note with a lipsticked imprint of your lips as a promise of kisses to come.

flirting, hugs, and *Holding* hands

I believe that it's important to show your partner physical affection no matter how long you've been together. In fact, the longer you're in a relationship, the more important these gestures become. Flirting comes naturally to us at the start of a relationship, but it's important to keep that spark alive as your life together continues. Here are some ways to keep in constant touch:

❖ Think back to the time that you first started dating. I'll bet you got butterflies in your stomach every time you saw him. Always keep that feeling in mind when you see him now.

❖ Go to a party where you spend most of the time circulating separately. But cross his path and give him a kiss or give his hand a quick squeeze or give him a wink of the eye.

❖ When you're across a crowded room or seated across from one another at a dinner party, make eye contact with him and hold his gaze, just like you would have done when you were first dating.

❖ Sneak up on him once in a while and hug him from behind.

❖ Act as if you're trying to win his heart— even though you know you already have.

❖ When you're out walking together, be sure to hold hands. And do it when you're sitting together in a movie or at the theater.

❖ Put your hand on his arm when you're speaking. Not only is it a warm, flirtatious gesture, it helps get your point across.

❖ In your day to day conversations and activities, be aware of moments where you can make a physical connection: If you're dining out, reach across the table and interlace your fingers as you peruse your menus; when you relax on the couch, intertwine your arms or take turns resting your feet on the other's lap.

❖ One couple I know has their own "secret connection." When they want to say "I love you" without words, they reach out and ever so briefly touch pointer fingers. Create your own "secret connection."

Showing Your *Appreciation* to Each Other

The things that you and your partner do for each other reaffirm your love and your commitment each day. These acts of kindness may range from the large to small, but it's important to acknowledge all of them. Avoid taking signs of love for granted by keeping these ideas in mind:

❖ It's important to thank your partner for everything he does, especially for the small things that might sometimes get overlooked, such as helping out around the house.

❖ Write your own top ten list of things you love best about your partner. Tape it to the bathroom mirror, or even mail it to him at the office to brighten up his day. Be sure to update it often!

❖ Be generous with your compliments about how he looks and what he does. If you think he's

the most wonderful man in the world, make sure he knows it!

❖ If you feel that your partner has been doing a lot for you lately, write him a card or letter that tells him how much you love him for it. We might not remember to say thank you for everything, but acknowledging his effort this way will make him feel very special.

❖ Always greet him with a smile and a kiss when you or he comes in from work. Even if your day has been a trying one, showing your appreciation and affection for your love sets a positive tone for the evening and helps your day end on an upbeat note.

❖ Instead of getting annoyed when he has to work late, realize he's doing it for the two of you and your family, and thank him for it. A bear hug or a back rub when he comes in will go a long way.

❖ When your love gives you a present, respond with heartfelt thanks. Even if it's not what you would have chosen for yourself, think of the time and effort he spent choosing something he thought would really please you. This sentiment alone should make you feel grateful. Remember that it's the thought that counts and not just what's inside the box.

Pampering YOURSELF

I don't think that we can care for other people if we don't care for ourselves. Pampering yourself on occasion isn't really a luxury, though it sounds like one. It's a necessity—a way of recharging our batteries and rejuvenating our spirit so that we can continue to give of ourselves to others. Fitting in these moments of serenity might be the only way we can hold onto our sanity sometimes. So, go ahead: Treat yourself well. Remember, there are many ways to give yourself "little escapes" without spending lots of money. Think about some of these ideas:

❧ Don't feel guilty about treating yourself to a small indulgence, such as a manicure or a pedicure, and don't save the latter just for summer. This is a pick-me-up that's good for your body and your mood.

❧ Get a massage. Swedish massage is very relaxing, and the oils the therapist uses can be mixed with aromatic essences for an extra uplifting effect. If you're uncomfortable with disrobing, try a shiatsu massage, which doesn't use oil and lets you wear loose clothing for the treatment. Drop a hint to your partner for a gift certificate.

THE MILL

❧ Curl up in loungewear that makes you feel special, such as silk pajamas or a beautiful robe. Don't think, "Oh, no one's looking, so what does it matter?" Your partner's looking. And, if you're anything like me, wearing beautiful things will make you feel romantic.

❧ Set aside some time just for yourself each and every week. It doesn't matter what you do with this time. You could take a tennis lesson, escape from the real world with a quiet walk in the park, work on your own personal projects, or watch a favorite television program. Bob and I often watch television in separate rooms after dinner. It sounds unromantic, but he doesn't like the same shows I do! This is time just for you.

❧ If you're running short on time, but it's your turn to make dinner, give yourself a break and order in. We can't do everything all the time.

❧ Take a personal day at work once or twice a year and spend it doing something you normally don't have time for.

❧ Dress up for no particular occasion. Wear an outfit that makes you feel wonderful, just because you want to.

❧ Run an aromatherapy bath for yourself (see "The Incurable Romantic: The Sensual Bath," page 132, for ideas).

Pampering your partner

Everyone loves to be spoiled. We can pamper ourselves, as we've just discussed, but there's something special about spoiling the one you love. Pampering your partner really means taking care of him, even in some small but thoughtful way. Here are some ways to make him feel special:

❖ Massage is always a treat. Buy some scented lotion or oil to try out, and experiment to find the ones he likes best. To truly spoil him, tell him that he gets to have massage on demand for a week.

❖ Let him sleep late on the weekend.

❖ Buy him some pampering self-care products, such as an after-shave balm. Many men are reluctant to go shopping for these items themselves but love using them when they have them.

❖ Frequently check online bookstores and preorder the next book or CD from his favorite writer or musical artist. Have it sent to him directly as a surprise.

❖ Sneak out on Saturday or Sunday morning and bring home his favorite bagels and the newspaper.

❖ If you don't know how to already, learn to fix his tie for him. You might do this before work sometimes, or make it part of your date-night ritual. If he's wearing cufflinks, fix them for him, too.

❖ Watch for the new issue of his favorite magazine to come out, and buy it for him before he realizes that it's available.

magical madrid

Madrid, the capital city of Spain, is one of the most romantic cities in the world. By European standards, it's very young: Before King Philip II permanently moved his royal court there in 1561, it was little more than a garrison, albeit one with a fantastic location, right in the center of the country. Madrid was built up during the time that Spain was at the height of its power in the sixteenth and seventeenth centuries, and its magnificence is a testimony to its rich past.

Madrid is one of the best cities in the world for art lovers. Its most famous museum, the Prado, boasts the best collection of Spanish art by the likes of Goya, Velázquez, and Murillo, though it also has excellent collections by other European masters such as El Greco, Rubens, Titian, Raphael, and Botticelli. Spain's monarchs

have long been art collectors. The Palacio Real, once the home of Spain's royal family, is a palace of mythic proportions, with two thousand rooms (not all open to the public!) filled with paintings by Velázquez, Goya, Rubens, El Greco, Juan de Flandes, and Caravaggio, among others, and frescos by Tiépolo. Sometimes Bob and I escape to these and the other beautiful museums of Madrid. We also love going to the bullfights, but I don't know if that counts as romantic!

It's not just grandeur that makes Madrid so special. The city has a rhythm all its own, a pulse as vital as the beat of flamenco music. Here's how you can bring some of the glorious warmth of Madrid into your life:

▶ Many Spaniards swear that cava, a sparkling white wine made in Spain, is as lovely as

Champagne. It's delicious and quite inexpensive—a good bottle will set you back only $10 or $15.

▶ The insistent rhythm of Spanish music can bring out the romantic in anyone. Spend an evening at a restaurant or club that plays Latin music. It's especially intoxicating if it's played live.

▶ Take some lessons together in Latin dance. You might think you have two left feet, but some of the dances are actually quite simple to learn—and you can put what you learn to good use in that Latin nightclub.

▶ Re-create the tradition of serving tapas—a variety of hot and cold Spanish hors d'oeuvres—at home. Tapas favorites include black olives, chèvre (goat cheese), chorizo (a slightly spicy sausage), hams, pickles, little omelettes, and other goodies baked in baby earthenware casseroles. Invented in the region of Spain called Andalusia, *tapa* means "cover." A saucer was customarily placed to cover a glass of fino, dry Spanish sherry, or draught beer to keep the little fruit flies from swarming in. A tidbit of food placed on the dish helped attract clients to the wine bar.

▶ Indulge in two traditions of Spain: the siesta (practically sacred in Spain) and eating late (dinner is typically served at 10:00 or 11:00 P.M.!) Take an afternoon nap on the weekend with your love and/or plan to eat out at a Spanish restaurant in your area—late!

▶ Rent one or two Spanish-language films for an evening. Pedro Almodavar is one of Spain's most renowned directors, if you're looking for a place to start.

❖ Breakfast in bed is a classic. But rather than leaving him with a tray of French toast and scrambled eggs, join him in bed for the meal (see "The Romantic Gourmet: Breakfast in Bed," page 151, for ideas).

❖ Buy tickets to a show or a comedy club, and take him out on the town for an evening.

❖ Occasionally run errands for him, such as dropping off shirts at the dry cleaners or picking up something he needs at the drugstore.

❖ If he missed a movie he wanted to see at the theater, rent it for him. On "movie night," serve up popcorn and other snacks he loves.

The Incurable Romantic
the *sensual* bath

My American friends swear by their showers, but like many Europeans, I am partial to taking baths. This isn't an exercise in efficiency but a wonderful way to relax body, mind, and spirit. Setting up your own sensual bath at home is easy—it's finding the time that can be a little harder. But it's well worth it: This is a treat that will soothe your soul while rejuvenating your spirit. Here's some bathtime lore and ideas for your own sensual bath:

❯ Great beauties of ancient times, such as Cleopatra, bathed in milk to beautify their complexions.

❯ During the Roman Empire, going to the public baths was a daily event for many people. Romans would soak in hot water, then jump into a cold bath, a technique still practiced in Scandinavia and Russia.

❯ Plan ahead so that there won't be any interruptions. This is your own private time, and you should enjoy it to the fullest. That means turning the ringer off the phone—and not feeling guilty about it.

❯ Run the water at a comfortably warm temperature, but don't let it get too hot, as this will dry out your skin.

❯ Buy a special bath oil or foam. You might try the same scent as your favorite perfume.

❯ Consider the relaxing powers of aromatherapy. Adding some lavender oil or a lavender-infused bath bomb, a sphere of powder that makes your bath effervescent, to your bath will soothe you; if you want to feel invigorated, use a product that contains juniper.

❯ Play some beautiful music. I like opera and New Zealand soprano Kiri Te Kanawa in particular. Classical music is another wonderful choice; I usually select something by Mozart or Rachmaninoff.

❯ Dim or turn off the overhead lights, and light a couple of votive candles. If you're not using a scented product in your bath, make sure to use a scented candle to infuse the room with a calming fragrance.

❯ Use a bath pillow or rolled towel to rest your head against in the tub; just be sure it's not so cozy that you fall asleep.

❯ Bring something to sip while you're soaking. A mug of herbal tea is lovely.

❯ Have a luxuriously plush towel ready for you to wrap yourself in when you emerge from the tub.

❯ Use a moisturizing lotion on your skin after your bath. Use a product with the same scent as your bath or one that is unscented so that it doesn't clash with the marvelous aroma.

SECRETS to Love: *Humility*

According to an old saying, "Pride goes before a fall." What that means is that pride is often responsible for a person's downfall, whether in public or private life. While taking pride in oneself is the cornerstone of self-esteem, know that there's a fine line between pride and arrogance, the attitude that you are always right—and others are always wrong when they challenge you.

Humility is the antidote to excessive pride. It is simply the quality of being humble, which is often defined as meekness. It doesn't sound very romantic, but it is a vital ingredient of love, for we cannot truly care for another if we maintain a prideful stance that fools us into thinking we are always right. How can love blossom in that atmosphere? True humility is not about becoming submissive; it's an asset to love. Here are some of the ways I think that humility fits into the romantic life:

❧ *Remember humility when you're in your partner's circle.* Sure, you might be able to spot the flaws of his friends and relatives, but is it really necessary to point them out to him? He probably already knows about them and has chosen to overlook them in his own way.

❧ *Remember humility when you have an argument.* One person can't fight alone; it always takes two. Think about the role you've played in creating the argument. One of the bravest things you can do is to take responsibility for helping resolve conflict.

❧ *Remember humility when you're convinced of your own rightness.* Your partner holds his views for a reason, and it's more important to respect his ideas than it is for you to convince him that you're always right.

❧ *Remember humility when you feel you're giving a great deal.* Pride so often carries with it expectations of reciprocity: "I've done X, so he should do Y." But the truth is that romance means giving of ourselves. Love shouldn't carry with it a balance sheet that you're constantly check-ing. Give your love because you want to give it.

elegant château lunch
du amour

The romantic lunch that Meredith and Luc enjoy in my novel Her Own Rules, *while staying at Luc's home in the Loire Valley, is the inspiration for this menu. The Loire river valley, known as "the garden of France," is renowned for its marvelous fruits and vegetables since the Middle Ages. This menu celebrates the best of the region's produce, including mushrooms, asparagus, and sun-ripened peaches, as well as farm-fresh goat cheese (chèvre).*

For a romantic and very French lunch, first serve the soup, then the omelet accompanied by the salad, and finish with a platter of classic French cheeses (see "The Romantic Gourmet: French Cheese Primer," page 138, for ideas.) Sliced bread, sliced red and green apples, and red grapes round out the platter. If you like, include crackers. (I like Carr's Table Water Crackers and Croissant Crackers.) Here are some inspirations to make your lunch special:

Menu

Creamy Asparagus Soup

Mushroom and Herb Omelet

Mixed Green Salad with Dijon Mustard Vinaigrette

Brie, French Blue, and Soft Mild Goat Cheese Served with Bread, Red Grapes, and Apples (see above)

Roasted Peaches Drizzled with Peach-Caramel Sauce

❖ There is something truly romantic about dining outdoors with nature as the backdrop. Serve the meal on a patio or underneath a beautiful tree in your backyard. Scatter fresh flower petals on the table and set it with your finest place mats and napkins.

❖ I use candlelight whenever I dine at home. At any time of the day, it adds a touch of romance. Place floating candles in a pretty bowl of water for a centerpiece.

❖ Music isn't only reserved for romantic dinners. Bob and I enjoy listening to music throughout the day. We love "The Three Tenors," Placido Domingo, Luciano Pavarotti, and José Carerras. They are undoubtedly the three most famous tenors in the world and have given some fabulous concerts together. If you dine outdoors, hide your portable stereo behind the tree!

❖ After lunch, rent a romantic French or American film. *Cousin, Cousine* and *Manon des Sources* (Manon of the Spring) are two very romantic films. For other suggestions of English-language films, see "The Incurable Romantic: The Ten Most Romantic Movies of All Time," page 165. When the movie is over, why not partake in a relaxing discussion about why it's a great love story.

Creamy Asparagus Soup

The stunning color and enticing fragrance of this soup will put you in a light-hearted springtime mood, even if it's the dead of winter. The rich, deep flavor of asparagus really comes through.

One 10-ounce package frozen asparagus
   spears, thawed
1 tablespoon butter
1 shallot, chopped
1 tablespoon all-purpose flour
Salt and freshly ground pepper
1³/4 cups vegetable or chicken broth
1 tablespoon heavy cream

1. Remove six 1¹/2-inch-long tips from the asparagus and set aside for garnish. Cut the remaining asparagus into 1-inch lengths.
2. Melt the butter in a medium saucepan over medium-low heat. Add the shallot and cook, stirring, for about 4 minutes, or until softened. Stir in the flour, a large pinch of salt, and a pinch of pepper; cook, stirring constantly, for 2 minutes. Add the asparagus and cook, stirring, for 1 minute longer.
3. Add the broth and bring the mixture to a boil over high heat. Reduce the heat to low and simmer for about 3 minutes, or until the asparagus is very tender when pierced with a fork.
4. Pour one-third of the mixture into a blender, cover (with the center part of the cover removed to let the steam escape) and

puree the mixture until smooth. Pour the puree through a coarse strainer into a bowl, pressing hard on the solids to extract all of the liquid. Repeat with the remaining asparagus mixture.

5. Return the puree to the saucepan and stir in the cream. Season with salt and pepper to taste; cook, stirring often, over medium-low heat, for 2 minutes, or just until heated through. If not serving immediately, let the soup come to room temperature, cover, and refrigerate for up to 1 day. Reheat gently before serving.

6. To serve, ladle the soup into bowls and garnish with the reserved asparagus tips.

Serves 2.

Mushroom and Herb Omelet

It's very French to have an omelet for lunch—and very romantic. Use whatever good-quality mushrooms are available or your favorites; any mushroom will be delicious. In the fall you might try porcini mushrooms, and in the spring fresh morels.

2 tablespoons butter
1 small onion, finely chopped
3 large white mushrooms (about 4 ounces), stems discarded and caps thinly sliced
1 tablespoon chopped fresh parsley
Salt and freshly ground black pepper
4 large eggs

1. Melt 1 tablespoon of the butter over medium-high heat in a heavy nonstick 10-inch skillet. Add the onion and cook, stirring occasionally, about 4 minutes, or until softened. Add the mushrooms, parsley, a large pinch of salt, and a pinch of pepper and cook, stirring occasionally, for about 4 minutes, or until the mushrooms soften. Transfer the mushroom mixture to a bowl and wipe the skillet clean.

2. Beat the eggs with $1/4$ cup water and $1/4$ teaspoon salt in a medium bowl. Melt $1 1/2$ teaspoons of the remaining butter over medium-high heat in the same skillet. Pour half of the egg mixture into the skillet and cook for about 1 minute, or until the eggs are set, gently lifting the edge of the eggs with a heat-safe rubber spatula and tilting the pan to allow the uncooked eggs to run underneath. Spoon half of the mushroom filling over half of the omelet. Fold the unfilled half of the omelet over the filling and slide the omelet onto a warm plate. Repeat with the remaining butter, egg mixture, and mushroom filling. Serve hot.

Serves 2.

Mixed Green Salad with Dijon Mustard Vinaigrette

If you want to prepare the salad greens a day ahead, just give them a wash and spin dry in a salad spinner, wrap them in damp paper towels, and store in self-sealing plastic bags in the refrigerator. You can also make the dressing in a jar with a tight-fitting lid; store it at room temperature. Or, be very French and make the salad dressing right in the serving bowl, top it with the greens, and then let the salad stand until time to serve: it's also very practical and doesn't result in a soggy salad. If you want to add other ingredients, like halved cherry tomatoes, matchstick-cut carrots or beets, or minced scallions, you can marinate them right in the dressing. And, sprinkling of warm toasted walnuts over the salad is quite wonderful, also.

I small shallot, minced

I teaspoon red wine vinegar

¹/₂ teaspoon Dijon mustard

Large pinch of salt

Pinch of freshly ground pepper

I tablespoon olive oil, preferably extra virgin

3 cups shredded romaine lettuce, washed
and spun dry

1. Whisk together the shallot, vinegar, mustard, salt, and pepper in a serving bowl. Add the oil in a slow, steady stream, whisking constantly; whisk until the vinaigrette is emulsified.

2. Place the romaine over the vinaigrette; cover and refrigerate, up to 3 hours.

3. Just before serving, toss the romaine with the vinaigrette; divide between chilled salad plates.

Serves 2.

c o u n t d o w n   t o   s u c c e s s

I Day Ahead

➡ Make the Creamy Asparagus Soup

➡ Make the Dijon Mustard Vinaigrette and
prepare the lettuce for Mixed Green Salad

I Hour Ahead

➡ Make the Roasted Peaches with Peach-
Caramel Sauce

15 Minutes Ahead

➡ Sauté the mushrooms for the Mushroom
and Herb Omelet

Roasted Peaches Drizzled with Peach-Caramel Sauce

If you don't feel like making caramel, use good-quality store-bought caramel sauce; warm it before adding the pureed peach. If the sauce seems too sweet, add squeezes of fresh lemon juice. Instead of the raspberries, you might sprinkle on crumbled peanut brittle: Use one tablespoon per serving.

3 firm-ripe peaches, peeled, halved, and pitted
6 tablespoons sugar
1/4 cup heavy cream
Raspberries, for garnish (optional)

1. Preheat the oven to 375°F. Place peaches, cut-side down, in a glass baking dish. Roast peaches for 20 minutes, or until softened.
2. Meanwhile, heat the sugar in a small heavy saucepan over medium heat, stirring with a fork until the sugar is dissolved Cook, swirling the pan occasionally, until the syrup turns golden brown. Quickly and carefully, stir in the cream and cook, stirring, until combined well.
3. Puree 2 of the peach halves in a food processor or blender until smooth. Stir the puree into the warm caramel sauce.
4. To serve, place two roasted peach halves, cut-side up, in each of two bowls (footed bowls, if you have them, are especially elegant), top each with about 2 tablespoons caramel sauce, and garnish with raspberries, if desired. Pass the remaining caramel sauce at the table.
Serves 2.

French Cheese PRIMER

France is a land of gourmets, and one of its most famous products is its cheese, of which there are more than seven hundred varieties. French cheese is famous the world over, and cheese making in France is regarded as a serious art. Cheese is made from the milk of cows, sheep, and goats, and the flavors run from creamy-mild to sharp and tart. On a label, "double crème" means that extra cream has been added to the cheese (approximately 35 percent butterfat) and that it has been aged for a longer time, producing a stronger, richer taste; "triple crème" means even more cream (approximately 75 percent butterfat)!

You might try hosting a wine-and-cheese party for two by buying small quantities of three or four of these cheeses and finding what most pleases your palate. Better cheese shops will be happy to let you taste samples in the store. Here are some popular French cheeses to begin with. Bon appetit!

▶ Beaufort. This is one of the oldest varieties of cheese in the world, dating back to ancient Roman times. The aging process takes four months, during which the cheese (made from the milk of the mahogany-colored Beaufort cows) is repeatedly rubbed with brine, making for a complex, salty taste when it matures.

▶ Brie. Made in the northeast of France, this double-crème, mild, soft cow's milk cheese is the best known French cheese and boasts the nickname "Queen of Cheeses." Records of Brie cheese making date back to A.D. 420. Its buttery, creamy flavor appeals to most palates. Look for the AOC (Appellation d'Origine Contrôlée) for an authentic Brie.

▶ Camembert. This cheese is made the world over, but connoisseurs believe that the only true Camembert is that made in Normandy. This soft cow's milk cheese is creamy-yellow in color, and its mild, delicately salty flavor goes well with just about anything. Camembert is named for a Norman village where there is a statue of its creator, Marie Harel. Legend has it that in 1855 one of her daughters gave Napoleon a piece of the cheese saying that it came from a village called Camembert. He ate it up and Camembert was born.

▶ Montrâchet. This is perhaps France's most famous chèvre, or goat's milk cheese. It's a creamy white cheese that has a recognizable but not overly strong flavor.

▶ Roquefort. If Brie is the "Queen," then Roquefort is the "King of Cheeses." Perhaps the most wonderful blue cheese in the world, Roquefort is made from ewe's milk and is ripened in the underground limestone caverns around Roquefort-sur-Soulzon. It's a strongly flavored hard cheese; if you find it too strong on its own, you might want to try crumbling a little over some endive leaves for a delicious salad.

▶ Saint-Agur. Made in the mountainous Auvergne region, this blue cow's milk cheese is milder than most other blue cheeses.

▶ Saint-André. This is actually Brie made with a triple-crème process—about as decadent as a cheese can get! Its unusual richness pairs up beautifully with Champagne, this is a personal favorite of mine. The crust should be white for a young cheese, beige for an older cheese, both of which are fine for consumption; watch out for a reddish-brown crust that sags in the middle, which indicates an overripe triple-crème cheese.

▶ Saint-Nèctaire. Also from Auvergne, this cheese is famous for its unusual aging process: The cheese is cured on a bed of straw for eight weeks. It boasts a fruity flavor and a lingering grassy aroma imparted by the hay.

creating a
Romantic
HOME

Your home is the stage on which your romantic life plays out. This is the place you are your true self, abandoning the barriers that you may put up to deal with the world. Home offers the armchair of intimacy and the hearth by which love warms itself. This is where you and your partner share your thoughts and dreams, and it must be a special place. While it is love that makes a house a home, you can enjoy finding the furnishings and fashioning the ambience to set the scene.

the *Romantic* HOME

*C*reating a romantic environment is about aesthetics and comfort. A room might be filled with dramatic designs and remarkable furniture, but if you can't relax in it, how romantic can you feel? Making a man feel comfortable makes him more romantic. I decorated the New York apartment that Bob and I share, and while I have certain preferences, such as for Art Deco and Biedermeier furniture, my plans have always been guided by a desire to create a warm, welcoming space. Let me share my six tenets for a romantic home:

❧ Your style is your own. Contemporary décor can be just as romantic as that of a country cottage; it's all in the details.

❧ Softness is a key to most rooms. Look for ways to soften straight lines in rooms, such as draperies at the windows and pillows on seating. Architectural elements like crown molding, chair rails, and overdoors also help soften a room, as do bookshelves or shelves used to display decorative objects.

❧ As much as possible, avoid using synthetic materials like plastic and polyester. Select natural products such as wood, glass, ceramics, cotton, and silk.

❖ Mix textures. You might think an all-white room looks cold, but if you blend textures, such as lace or sheer white curtains, a thick cashmere throw, and damask, linen, or matelassé bed linens, your bedroom becomes a romantic haven.

❖ Don't be afraid of color. My dining room walls are raspberry red; I have a small sitting room decorated entirely in shades of blue and white; the décor of my library is based on a color scheme of parchment-colored walls and pink, blue, and yellow fabrics. Color fosters emotions and adds beauty everywhere. If a certain color makes you feel good, or even makes you smile, than it's a good choice for you.

❖ Don't overdo. Like any good artist, know when to stop. Overloading a room tends to make it look cluttered, even messy, and reduces the sense of space. Always edit accessories.

the living room

❖ Pillows are one of the best investments you can make in a living room, and they're much less expensive than buying new furniture! You can spend a fortune or you can seek out amazing knock-offs in discount home furnishing outlets. Pillows covered in velvet, brocade, or silk are luxurious to the touch; scatter them liberally on sofas and armchairs.

❖ Framed photographs of you, your partner, and loved ones add a personal note as well as style to the living room. I keep photographs in almost every room! Choose an unusual spot to group photos together in a "mini-gallery." I have a grouping on an antique Biedermeier secretary in my living room, including a cherished photo of Winston Churchill given to me by his granddaughter. You might place them atop a piano or a small shelf made of crown molding on a wall.

❖ Books have always been important to me and I like to have them all around me. You can stack three or four art books on a coffee table, ottoman, or small desk. Ask for lushly illustrated "coffee table" books on travel, history, and artists or photogra-

phers as gifts for Christmas or your birthday; scour secondhand bookstores for used editions as well as the bargain-books section of larger bookstores, but only buy those in good condition.

❖ Perhaps the single most romantic element you can have in a living room is a fireplace. If you're lucky enough to have one, use it! Fill it with votives or a wrought iron candleholder that holds pillar candles in the warmer months. If you don't have a fireplace, consider adding hearth-inspired decorations in a few places, such as a basket or two of natural pinecones.

❖ Use the living room to display a favorite collection, but make sure it has an artistic aesthetic. Someone I know keeps an exquisite collection of marble eggs and hand-painted wooden eggs from Poland in two pedestal bowls that belonged to her grandmother. She used to take them out just at Easter, but I encouraged her to keep them on display year round. Teapots form one of my favorite collections, and especially important is an antique teapot that was given as a wedding present to my parents in the 1920s.

❖ Draperies and window treatments soften the edges of windows and add a fabulous ambience to the romantic home. Look for unusual or ornate poles and tiebacks. Be as creative as your budget allows.

the dining room

❖ While you might keep your dining table bare day to day, especially if it has a beautiful finish, experiment with tablecloths for special occasions to dress up a weeknight dinner. Look in home design magazines, tear out examples you like, and start a table setting file for inspiration.

❖ Don't skimp on candles. In addition to providing the perfect light to dine by (see "Candles and Lighting," page 147, for ideas), they add a touch of romance.

❖ Many people own lovely objects—figurines, Russian nesting dolls, vases, decorative plates, silvery mercury glass—that rarely see the light of day because they remain in storage for protection. I believe

in enjoying things, and the dining table or sideboard are wonderful places to display precious objects as centerpieces.

❖ Look for unusual objects for the dining table too. For example, I recently fell in love with some red and blue heart-shaped paperweights designed by Elsa Peretti for Tiffany. When I saw them at a dinner party where the hostess gave them as party favors, I admired them tremendously. Bob bought some for me as a surprise, and now I use them as table decorations for dinner parties along with clear crystal decorative objects I already had. Don't get caught up in what an item is "supposed" to do; if you find it beautiful, think of a way to add it to your table.

❖ Even if you didn't inherit Great Aunt Agatha's fine china, look for one or two unusual pieces to add a romantic and historical accent to the table. Some ideas include: a gilt or floral-edged serving platter; salt cellars, which are individual salt bowls with tiny spoons; an antique salt and pepper set; serving tongs; a set of silver dessert forks; napkin rings.

the bedroom

❖ Look for unusual containers such as a ceramic pitcher or antique bowl, in addition to vases, to fill with flowers. Set one on your nightstand or dresser.

❖ Cover a small round table with a floral-patterned fabric or two layered fabrics to give the room a fresh, romantic look. If your bedroom is small, consider this type of table instead of a nightstand on one side of the bed.

❖ Just as extra pillows add visual interest, softness, and comfort to the living room, they work the same way in the bedroom. Stock up on decorative pillows in different sizes—the European square, boudoir, and neckroll—to complement your bed linens. Use antique linen pillowcases and display them on top of the bed to add charm.

❖ Fragrance can help turn the bedroom into a serene space for the two of you. I always use potpourri, and I am very partial to Slatkin & Co.'s "Wisteria & Lilac" potpourri (available through www.neimanmarcus.com and www.amenwardy.com). I also favor Kenneth Turner of London's "Bramble Walk" room cologne (available through 1-800-405-6841).

❖ Keep framed photographs of yourself and your partner in your bedroom. This isn't the place for snapshots of others, even your beloved children. This is private space for the two of you.

❖ Keep a volume or two of poetry or romantic prose on your nightstand as a reminder to read to your partner. Display hardcover volumes that are beautifully bound—try secondhand bookstores for these.

the bathroom

❖ It's very romantic to create the feel of a lush hotel bathroom. Keep quality cotton bathrobes on hand. Luxurious towels are a must: Fold them in thirds lengthwise, roll, and display them in a gorgeous basket or on an old platter.

❖ Instead of a bathroom closet, consider storing toiletries and towels in a narrow wooden armoire or a "distressed" chest of drawers. In the house we once owned in Connecticut, I used an antique cradle to store a selection of rolled towels. Also, a cradle makes a great repository for magazines, if the bathroom is large enough.

❖ If you're feeling daring, paint the bathroom a rich, dark hue like plum or burgundy—even the ceiling.

❖ Put up a print of one of Renoir's beautiful bathers or another painting that conjures up a romantic scene for you.

❖ For romantic lighting, forget the overhead fixture or buy a vintage one. Use a floor lamp, small table lamps on a small, marble-topped antique table, and wall sconces.

❖ Scented candles are a must. I also recommend scented hand and bath soaps.

❖ Display bath foams and gels in beautiful bottles by the side of the bath. If your favorite doesn't come in a pretty bottle, find one at a home furnishings store in colored or clear glass or ceramic and pour in the gel with a small funnel.

Looking at art is truly a passion of mine. And that's one reason I made Laura Valiant, the main character of A *Sudden Change of Heart*, a partner in an art dealership. Standing in front of a painting that is centuries old can be mesmerizing, and I appreciate the artist's vision and the emotions or memories the painting evokes. A painting does not have to be that of a love scene to be romantic; in fact, some of the most beautiful works of art I can think of are landscapes.

▶ My favorite landscape artist is the world-famous J. M. W. Turner, also a wonderful seascape artist. I have always been awed by the way he captured light on canvas so magnificently. The National Gallery and the Tate Gallery in London hold most of his works. It was my mother who first took me to the Tate to see Turner's paintings.

▶ Before the advent of photography, paintings were the only visual record of a person. I admire the work of the great seventeenth- and eighteenth-century portraitists such as Sir Peter Lely, Sir Thomas Gainsborough (see painting, left), and Sir George Romney. In my novel *Voice of the Heart*, I included a Gainsborough portrait of lead character Francesca Avery's great-great-great-great grandmother in my description of Francesca's exquisite London apartment and a Romney portrait of the same ancestor at the family's Yorkshire castle.

▶ The Impressionists, who earned their name in late-nineteenth-century France for paintings that represented the effect of light upon a subject, are another personal favorite. I admire Renoir most, but also Gauguin, Van Gogh, Chagall, Manet, and Sisley.

▶ I also admire the pre-Raphelites, especially Dante Gabriel Rossetti and Edward Burne-Jones. Dating back to England in 1848, these painters were true romantics, finding beauty, love, and truth in dark forests and scenes of social distress. They are known as pre-Raphaelites because they painted "nothing but the truth," rebelling against the painters of the high Renaissance who "embellished" truth, reshaping the world, God, and life in their paintings. The Tate Gallery holds many Rossetti and Burne-Jones paintings.

Candles
and Lighting

*B*ob and I dine in candlelight every single night, even when we're alone. Here are some ways to create an atmosphere of romance with beautiful lighting effects:

❖ I recommend scented candles. My favorites are made by Kenneth Turner of London. I use the original scent, which comes in its own container with a "bee" lid, and whenever I smell them I know I'm home! Another candle I love is called "White Flowers," which is made by Slatkin & Co.

❖ Experiment with different types of candles; there are dozens. I prefer tapers in the dining room, but sometimes I use the delicate little tea lights or votive candles. Thick column candles, sometimes called "pillars," in different heights, make for interesting arrangements too. Decide what styles feel the most romantic to you. In the dining room, keep the maximum candle height about two inches below eye level, so no one's view is blocked.

❖ Candleholders come in every shape, style, and material imaginable. I know someone whose dining room has no electric lights but rather a wrought-iron candle chandelier, a brass candelabra, and a pair of wrought-iron sconces on the wall. Dining there makes you feel like you're in a medieval castle—marvelous!

❖ Trim your wick properly: If a wick is too long, the candle will smoke, and this can discolor walls and ceilings; if the wick's too short, the candle won't burn properly. After each use, let the wick cool briefly, then trim to one-quarter inch.

❖ Get rid of the "new" look of your candles by burning them down about an inch before the first use.

❖ Use a long-handled candle snuffer to put out your candles. Not only does a brass or silver one evoke the charm of yesteryear, it reduces the chance of blowing sparks, soot, or wax onto the surface surrounding the candle.

❖ A dimmer switch lets you adjust the level of lighting for romantic dining. In addition to dimmers, you might look for lamps that accommodate a three-way bulb.

❖ Dress up some of your lamps with decorative shades, which you can buy separately. These are available in romantic colors, patterns, and materials, and some have wonderful details, such as tassels or fringe.

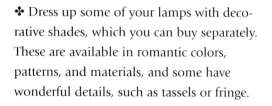

Flowers

I have fresh flowers all over my home and feel very lucky that my husband makes a custom of bringing me flowers every Friday or sometimes on Saturday. Flowers add a romantic touch, whether displayed in a generous bouquet, simple nosegay, or dramatic single bloom.

❖ Many people believe that red roses spell romance, but I've never been partial to them. I am fond of peonies and white or pastel roses, and I absolutely love white orchids. Decide what your own preferences are, and use those blooms around your home. Don't ever feel obligated to choose certain flowers just because they're conventionally considered romantic.

❖ While a large bouquet of flowers feels lushly romantic, try using one or two perfect blooms on their own.

❖ Flowers always look beautiful, but not all of them have a fragrance. Keep this in mind when you're shopping for them.

the most romantic spot in new york

To me, Central Park is magical at all times of the year. Considered the world's most famous park, it's an 843-acre oasis in the middle of Manhattan where you can forget about the hustle and bustle of the city that never sleeps. The trees block the traffic noise, and soon all is forest foliage, chirping birds, and the sound of laughter.

Created in the mid-1850s, Central Park was the first landscaped public park in the United States, its development driven by wealthy merchants and landowners who believed that beautiful public grounds like those in London and Paris would help New York garner an international reputation. The park would also create an attractive setting for carriage rides and give working-class New Yorkers a healthy alternative to the saloon. Here are some of my favorite parts of the park:

❱ Bob and I often dine out at Tavern on the Green, the stunning restaurant at the center of the park. (The "At-Home Supper for the Incurable Romantic" menu, page 153, is inspired by Tavern on the Green's wonderful menu.)

❱ Taking a horse-and-carriage ride in the park, a charming nod to the past, is the epitome of romance. You can take a ride any time of year, but there's a special charm in the fall and winter, when brightly colored leaves or a fresh dusting of snow cover the ground.

❱ The Conservatory Garden, on the east side (enter at Fifth Avenue and 105th Street), is a six-acre horticultural gem with gardens designed in the European tradition.

❱ Shakespeare in the Park is a summer program of free plays featuring renowned actors at the park's Delacorte Theater.

❱ The beautiful carousel (midpark at 64th Street) first opened in 1871, powered by a blind mule and a horse that walked a treadmill in an underground pit. The carousel that stands today features some of the largest hand-carved jumping horses in the United States.

Outside your *Home*

We're used to decorating the rooms of our homes, but I like to think about the open air spaces beyond our doors as "rooms" too. Here are some ways to add romance to the outside of your home, even if you live in an apartment.

❖ Ask for advice at a garden center to help you create a simple garden from low-maintenance plant varieties. Include some flowers that you can cut; there's no more romantic floral arrangement than one from your own garden. Include a focal point, such as a sundial or sculpture.

❖ Place a loveseat or two Adirondack chairs under a tree or hang a swing seat or hammock from a strong branch to beckon the two of you on a lazy afternoon.

❖ Fill stone, ceramic, or terra cotta planters with flowering plants to add color as well as soften the corners of your patio or deck.

❖ Hang Japanese paper lanterns or string up miniature white lights for a festive atmosphere every night.

❖ Turn your balcony into a cozy "outdoor room" and "decorate" liberally with lush flower boxes and colorful potted plants.

❖ Create a potted herb garden on your deck or balcony. Rosemary, basil, and thyme require little maintenance. Enjoy their fragrance, and use them in your cooking.

❖ Enjoy your own private café—wrought-iron tables and chairs add instant romance. Even a tiny balcony has room for a small bistro table and chairs. Dine al fresco whenever you can. It is so romantic to eat breakfast outdoors and linger over coffee.

❖ Decorate your front door with a wreath for each season, not just at Christmas. Display a heart-shaped wreath in February. A spring wreath might include silk or fresh flowers and pastel satin ribbon. A fall wreath can be fashioned from a bent twig or grapevine base, eucalyptus, and dried berries or hydrangeas.

❖ Classical symmetry is romantic. Place identical planters, each with a miniature pine tree, on each side of the doorway.

❖ Your entryway can double as a garden. Use hanging planters and potted flowering plants, or plant a colorful border along the front edge.

Breakfast
in BED

Breakfast in bed is the ultimate indulgence. I rarely partake of it because book deadlines and appointments get in the way, but that just makes me appreciate the luxury of it all the more, for example, when I'm traveling and ordering room service. Preparing a meal for your partner is always a symbol of love, but breakfast in bed is uniquely special.

▶ Keep it simple. There's no need to get up at 5:00 A.M. to start cooking an elaborate breakfast. Pancakes, eggs, bacon, toast, and cut-up fresh fruit are easy to make and taste delicious. To save time, try recipes that you can assemble the night before, refrigerate, and bake in the oven in the morning, like strata, a delicious breakfast dish made of layered bread, egg, crumbled sausage, and grated cheese.

▶ Here are some more make-ahead tips: Prepare muffin batter the night before and refrigerate, covered; prepare scrambled egg and milk mixture the night before (but do not add seasonings, meats, or vegetables until right before cooking) and refrigerate.

▶ Add a few culinary surprises. If your husband loves scrambled eggs, try mixing them with chèvre (goat cheese), wild mushrooms, diced smoked salmon, or fresh herbs for added flavor. Or choose a different preserve to go with toast: Instead of strawberry jam, try black currant, an English classic, or ginger-flavored marmalade.

▶ Use a pretty tray to serve the meal. I love a traditional silver breakfast tray, but another lovely option is to use a simple wicker tray. Tie some colorful ribbon around the handles for a soft touch. And if you're worried that a vase of flowers will tip over too easily, cut the flower stems short and place in a small, shallow bowl or a pretty ceramic creamer.

▶ For the perfect hotel flourish, create your own room service. Design and make a menu with a choice of items you know your partner loves, but make sure your pantry and refrigerator are stocked with all the right ingredients. When you wake up, hand your partner the menu. Prepare the "order" and present it on an elegantly set breakfast tray. Don't forget a bud vase with one single stem and the morning newspaper. Just like a four-star hotel!

The Romantic Gourmet

SECRETS to Love: *Compassion*

When things are going well, we feel that we can handle anything, but when we're down, compassion can truly heal and revive our spirits. Compassion is a deeply thoughtful awareness of the suffering of another person, combined with a desire to ease his pain. It's a quality we may not think about expressing every day, but in fact, compassion does play an important role in our daily lives.

Compassion requires us to step outside ourselves to look with no bias upon our partner, and try to feel, or at least imagine, what difficulties he is experiencing. Showing compassion is a way of supporting your partner, helping him remember he is not alone. It takes a great deal of strength and courage to really be a compassionate person, but doing so will strengthen your relationship immeasurably and move it to a higher level.

❖ *Show compassion through words and deeds.* You can be actively compassionate by making time to tune into your partner regularly, by asking "How are you?" and really listening to his answer, by expressing your interest in helping him work out issues, by thinking about ways to make his life easier when he's under duress, or just by giving him a long, warm hug to remind him you're there, even if he doesn't feel like talking.

❖ *Show compassion by giving your partner space.* While we may want to solve our partner's problems for him, we sometimes have to step back and accept that all we can offer is support, not answers. Being compassionate means being there for him but also giving him space to make his own decisions.

❖ *Show compassion even when you're angry.* It's a very human thing for a person to lash out at a partner when things aren't going well. It's a sad fact that sometimes we're harshest to those we love the most because we think: "It's safe; he'll love me no matter what." If things get heated, tell your partner that you'll talk later and that you are willing to listen to anything he has to say.

❖ *Look for ways for you and your partner to express compassion as a couple.* Choose a cause to volunteer your time to, set aside a small part of your budget to make a donation to a cause you believe in, give blood, or pay a visit to a troubled friend. Showing your compassion as a couple reinforces compassionate behavior with each other.

at-home supper for the incurable romantic

This menu was inspired by the scene in my novel A Secret Affair, *when Bill, his daughter Helena, his mother Drucilla, and Vanessa meet at the famous Tavern on the Green—Central Park at West 67th Street in New York—to celebrate the holiday season. Tavern on the Green opened in 1934 with a coachman in full regalia at the door. Chef Gary Coyle kindly shared his recipes, which we adapted for this menu. Here are some romantic suggestions for your dinner:*

❖ I like to get dressed elegantly on certain occasions when I go out with Bob. You can do the same in your own home. Don your best outfit, do your hair, and spray on your favorite fragrance, just as if you were going out to an elegant restaurant.

❖ Use your best china—don't hide it away. Use antique table linens and vintage silver-plate flatware. If your budget is limited, remember, you only need two settings. Light elegant candles, such as tall white tapers, and buy fresh flowers for your table—miniature white roses or fragrant lilies.

❖ Hire a calligrapher or use your best script to write the dinner menu on elegantly designed stationery, and place it in a beautiful frame to display on the table.

❖ Before dinner is served, make your loved one's favorite cocktail and slow dance to Frank Sinatra. One of our favorite Sinatra songs to dance to is "One for My Baby, One More for the Road."

❖ Tavern on the Green's wine director, Spiro Baltas, recommends serving a dry white wine, such as Franz Hirtzberger Grüner Veltliner, with the salad course and Gary Farrell Pinot Noir or Chalk Hill Sauvignon Blanc with the main course; however, any pinot noir or sauvignon blanc will go well with these dishes.

Menu

Mesclun with Lemon Vinaigrette and Cherry Tomatoes

Crab Cakes with Avocado Tartar Sauce

Tavern on the Green Fennel Slaw

Strawberry "Sweet Nothings" Shortcakes with Strawberry Coulis

Mesclun with Lemon Vinaigrette and Cherry Tomatoes

Chef Gary Coyle suggests that you might also add thinly sliced red onions, crisp toasted croutons, marinated fresh mozzarella, or goat cheese medallions to this simple but superb salad. Serve it as a first course, before the crab cakes and fennel slaw.

1/2 teaspoon finely grated lemon zest

1 tablespoon fresh lemon juice

3 fresh basil leaves, very finely shredded

1 garlic clove, minced

1/4 teaspoon salt

Pinch of freshly ground pepper

3 tablespoons olive oil

1/2 pint yellow and/or red cherry or grape tomatoes, halved

3 cups mesclun, washed and spun dry

2 tablespoons snipped fresh chives

1. Whisk together the lemon zest and juice, basil, garlic, salt, and pepper in a small bowl. Add the oil in a slow, steady stream, whisking constantly, until blended. The vinaigrette can be prepared ahead and stored, covered, at room temperature, for up to 4 hours. Whisk well before using.

2. Place the tomatoes in a small bowl and toss with 2 tablespoons of the vinaigrette. Let stand at room temperature for at least 10 minutes or up to 30 minutes.

3. Just before serving, toss the mesclun and chives with the remaining 2 tablespoons vinaigrette until well coated. Arrange the mesclun on salad plates, spoon the tomatoes around the edges, and serve.

Serves 2.

Tavern on the Green

Crab Cakes with
Avocado Tartar Sauce

Crispy, delicate and slightly sweet with a luscious, rich texture,
these just might become your favorite recipe for a romantic meal.

1/2 cup mayonnaise

1 large egg white

1 teaspoon chopped fresh parsley

1 teaspoon chopped fresh cilantro

1 teaspoon fresh lemon juice

Large pinch of salt

Pinch of cayenne pepper

1 pound lump crabmeat, picked over to
remove shells and cartilage

1/3 cup dry bread crumbs

Avocado Tartar Sauce (recipe follows)

1. Preheat the oven to 400°F. Lightly oil
   a baking sheet.

2. Whisk together the mayonnaise, egg white,
   parsley, cilantro, lemon juice, salt, and
   cayenne in a medium bowl. Gently fold
   in the crabmeat and bread crumbs with a
   rubber spatula, mixing just until combined.

3. Gently form the crab mixture into four
   1-inch-thick cakes. The crab cakes can
   be prepared ahead to this point. Cover
   and refrigerate for up to 4 hours. Bring
   to room temperature before baking.

4. Place crab cakes on prepared baking sheet.
   Bake 15 to 20 minutes, until golden brown.

5. Transfer the crab cakes to serving plates,
   top each with a spoonful of Avocado

Tartar Sauce, and serve immediately.
   Pass the remaining sauce separately.
Serves 2.

Avocado Tartar Sauce

The chef recommends adding a squeeze of
anchovy paste or a bit of minced anchovy to
the sauce, if you're a fan.

1 tablespoon chopped fresh parsley

1 tablespoon chopped cornichon
   (I favor Dessaux–brand cornichons) or
   gherkin

1 tablespoon chopped shallot

1/4 avocado, peeled and pitted

1 teaspoon fresh lemon juice

1/4 cup mayonnaise

Salt and freshly ground pepper

With the motor running, add the parsley,
cornichon, and shallot to a food processor
and process until finely chopped. Add the
avocado and lemon juice and process until
the avocado is smooth. Transfer to a bowl
and stir in the mayonnaise; season with
salt and pepper to taste. The sauce can be
prepared ahead. Cover and refrigerate for
up to 3 hours.

Tavern on the Green
Fennel Slaw

Crisp and refreshing, this salad is great with just about any casual meal, but it is especially wonderful served alongside Tavern on the Green's fabulous crab cakes.

Tavern on the Green

1 tablespoon mayonnaise

1 slender scallion, minced

1 teaspoon red wine vinegar

1 teaspoon sugar

1/4 teaspoon celery seeds

Large pinch of salt

Pinch of freshly ground pepper

1 medium fennel bulb, trimmed and
   cut into 1/4-inch-thick strips

1/2 cup matchstick-cut carrots

1. Stir together the mayonnaise, scallion, vinegar, sugar, celery seeds, salt, and pepper in a small bowl. The dressing can be prepared ahead. Cover and refrigerate for up to 3 hours.
2. Just before serving, toss the dressing with the fennel and carrots in a medium bowl until well combined. *Serves 2.*

c o u n t d o w n   t o   s u c c e s s

1 Day Ahead

➡ Make the Strawberry Coulis

4 Hours Ahead

➡ Prepare the crab cakes through step 3

➡ Make the Lemon Vinaigrette

3 Hours Ahead

➡ Make the dressing for the fennel slaw

➡ Make the Avocado Tartar Sauce

1 Hour Ahead

➡ Bake the biscuits for the strawberry shortcake

Strawberry "Sweet Nothings" Shortcakes with Strawberry Coulis

If you like, use a pastry bag and a half-inch star tip to pipe the whipped cream over the strawberries, just like the pastry chef does at Tavern on the Green.

1 cup all-purpose flour
3 tablespoons plus 1 teaspoon granulated sugar
3/4 teaspoon baking powder
Pinch of salt
1 1/4 cups heavy cream
1 tablespoon confectioners' sugar
1 cup fresh strawberries, hulled and sliced
Strawberry Coulis (recipe follows)

1. Position a rack in the middle of the oven and preheat to 375°F.
2. Whisk together the flour, 3 tablespoons of the granulated sugar, the baking powder, and salt in a small bowl.
3. Whip 3/4 cup of the cream in a large bowl with an electric mixer on medium-high speed just to stiff peaks. Sift the dry ingredients over the whipped cream and blend with a rubber spatula just until a dough forms (do not overmix).
4. Knead the dough, with lightly floured hands, in the bowl, until it just comes together, about 8 times. On a lightly floured surface, divide the dough in half, and form each piece into a disk about 3-inches round and 1-inch thick. Transfer the disks to an ungreased baking sheet and sprinkle each with 1/2 teaspoon of the remaining granulated sugar.

5. Bake the shortcakes for 25 minutes, or until golden brown. Transfer the shortcakes to a wire rack and let cool. The shortcakes can be baked up to 1 hour ahead.
6. Just before serving, whip the remaining 1/2 cup cream and the confectioners' sugar in a large bowl with an electric mixer on medium-high speed just to stiff peaks.
7. To serve, slice each biscuit horizontally in half with a serrated knife and place the bottom halves on dessert plates. Spoon the strawberries over the shortcakes, drizzle with the Strawberry Coulis, and top with the whipped cream. Cover with the biscuit tops and serve.

Serves 2.

Strawberry Coulis

1 cup fresh strawberries, hulled and sliced
1 tablespoon confectioners' sugar, or as needed, depending on sweetness of berries

Puree the strawberries with the sugar in a food processor. Pour mixture through a fine strainer set over a bowl, pressing hard on the solids to extract all the liquid. The sauce can be prepared ahead. Cover and refrigerate for up to 1 day.

Makes about 1/2 cup.

the Romance of a Lifetime

As your relationship grows, so does your capacity for romance. I think it's a case of the more you have, the more you want, and the more you give, the more you reap. Romance is addictive. After all, it makes us feel as if we're on top of the world. As time goes by, treasure the memories you share and cherish the moments you have together. Those memories and moments interlock to forge a bond that builds and inspires a deeper, more enduring love between you and your partner.

finding Romantic *Inspirations*
to make LOVE last

*B*ecause I've been married thirty-eight years to the same man, I am often asked, "What's the secret to your long marriage?" I like to tease, saying it's because Bob travels a lot! And it's true, we all need space in our togetherness, but I do believe it is entirely possible to keep romance alive in a relationship over the years. However, what many people don't recognize is that it does take some effort because, as a partnership continues over time, the risk is that it can fall into a kind of comfortable rut.

Sometimes I am saddened when I see a couple who are just not "doing the work." They may be great people as individuals, but their relationship is unraveling and weakening because they don't make a sustained, concerted effort to stay connected, to work out differences, to keep things interesting and new, to plan joyful things to look forward to, and to remind each other what they mean to each other. It's important to reflect on where you've been, where you are now, and where you're going together.

I saw a quote once by the writer Ursula K. Le Guin that resonated with me: "Love just doesn't sit there, like a stone, it has to be made, like bread; re-made all the time, made new." A relationship is a dynamic, ever-changing entity, not a static state of being. Commit to working on the relationship together to continually polish and bring out its warm tones, smooth away any rough edges that develop, and nurture its joyful qualities every day. Here are some ideas to get you started:

❖ Work toward a goal together. Make a plan for your ideal home or your fantasy vacation, then write down the steps you'll need to take to make it happen. Decide between the two of you who will do what: One of you might research realtors or take books out of the library about your dream destination. Decide, too, what you'll do together: visit potential neighborhoods or meet with a travel agent. When possible, establish a time frame for each step, not to add the pressure of a deadline but to keep the plan moving and real. You can always change an interim date. The challenge and reward of making a dream come true will bind you more closely together.

❖ Don't be afraid to try something new, whether it is cooking an elaborate meal, volunteering for a cause you care about deeply, or simply taking up a new sport. Expanding your horizons only creates more space in which love can flourish.

❖ Read voraciously. I read many of the papers from England and those published in New York. Know what's new, what's interesting, and what's happening. An art exhibit opening, a controversial movie, a significant development on the political front—that's what makes for interesting conversation. Men want to talk to women who are connected to the outside world, who have information and opinions, who bring something new to the conversation.

❖ Reread your old love letters. Be warned: This can bring out a torrent of emotion! When you're done, write your spouse a new one.

❖ Revisit a place that has special meaning to you. It might be the place where you first said "I love you," or the café where you got engaged, or the country inn where you enjoyed that memorable getaway. Wherever it is, return to it on occasion. Not only will the trip stir up tender feelings, but it will let you reflect on how your love has grown.

❖ Do you remember what you did during the first year you dated—what music you listened to or what films you watched? Bring out those CDs or videos and experience them again. You'll bring back wonderful memories.

❖ Remind yourself to savor every moment. Too often we think about the things we wish we had or could have. Yes, it's important to plan for the future, but make a conscious effort to savor the precious gift of your love every day. We only have today; we don't know what tomorrow will bring.

❖ Remember all of the reasons that you fell in love with your partner in the first place. Write a list and leave it somewhere where your spouse will find it.

❖ When you're reminiscing, don't forget the troubled waters you've crossed together. Overcoming adversity strengthens your partnership. Tell your partner about a time when his support helped your relationship.

the power of *Spontaneity*

*W*e've discussed surprises, as in you know what's going to happen— the surprise is for your partner to discover. Spontaneity is a different quality altogether, because you can surprise yourself, too. It means giving in to some of your impulses and adopting a playful, irreverent attitude.

❖ Say "I love you" first. Say it many times and say it for no reason at all.

❖ Be open to the possibilities around you. If you see an announcement for an unusual event in the paper or read a review of a film

or a play that really interests and excites you, tell your partner that you're taking him out for the night. Don't tell him where, and go see it.

❖ Spontaneity doesn't mean that you have to rush and do something immediately. It's very romantic to make a decision spontaneously and then work out the logistics later. Last year, I told Bob, "I'm going to take you to Paris for your birthday." It was just this wonderful idea that came to me suddenly, and he was thrilled about it. Of course, it was a memorable trip—and it all began with a whim.

❖ Wake up one morning and decide to spend a day together without an itinerary. Just get into the car and drive, and stop wherever you want to along the way. Perhaps you could bring along a picnic lunch to enjoy in a perfect, secluded spot you discover, or you could end up eating at a country inn that you never knew existed. Just go with your instincts!

❖ When you think of your lover during the day, give him a quick call or e-mail to let him know. Short and sweet is perfect for a quick message.

❖ If an opportunity to do something interesting comes up, grab it. You might get a last-minute invitation to a party or an event, or take an impromptu trip, which often can be had for a song. Don't feel that you need to plan everything in advance.

❖ Laugh aloud. There is something musical about the sound of laughter, and having a sense of humor about things helps enhance your spontaneous side.

❖ Play a board game together as if you were kids. Use a perennial favorite like Monopoly or Scrabble. Playing games—childhood favorites—can bring out a spontaneous side you forgot was there.

❖ If your partner makes a suggestion that sounds silly to you, check your reaction. Trust him and let him reveal his spontaneous side, too.

captivating capri

For centuries, the island of Capri, which lies just off the coast of Italy near Naples and Sorrento, and is only accessible by boat, has captivated everyone—from ancient emperors to many young lovers. Octavian Augustus, the Roman emperor, lived here, as did his successor Tiberius, who created charming villas around the island, of which the ruins of three remain: Villa Jovis, Sea Palace, and Damecuta. Tiberius loved the island so much that he left it for Rome only when it was absolutely necessary.

The *faraglioni* (crags), probably Capri's best known attraction, are high, sheer cliffs that have been strongly eroded by the sea and wind, creating sections isolated from the mainland. Capri is perhaps most famous, however, for the *Grotto Azzura* (Blue Grotto), an unforgettable cave in water about sixty feet deep and filled with radiant blue light.

While I am always dazzled by the sites of Capri, what I love most about the island is its relaxed attitude. Some friends of ours invited Bob and me to join them for a sail down the Italian coastline to Capri; that lovely trip captured all that is wonderful about this beautiful place. No one rushes about in a mad dash, desperate to get to the next appointment or meeting (though they do take the hairpin curves on the road to the town of Anacapri very fast!). Instead life is savored at a slower pace. I enjoy sitting at the unpretentious La Capannina restaurant or the Quisisana Hotel and just watching the world go by. Here are some ways to enjoy Capri's spirit:

◗ A visit to Capri must include dining al fresco in one the *trattorias*, such as those that flank the Piazza Umberto I in the resort town of Capri, the island's main town. Take your partner to an outdoor café. Don't forget to people-watch, another Italian pastime.

◗ Try some *limoncello*, a liqueur made from the wealth of lemon trees on Capri. Limoncello is a blend of lemon zest, alcohol, sugar, and herbs. It can be enjoyed on its own or mixed with vodka as a cocktail.

◗ Spend an evening with friends. Life on Capri is convivial—this is a café culture, remember. Get together with one or two other couples for a lively night on the town.

Renewing your *Commitment*

*I*n many cultures, a wedding is the one, and often only, way for a couple to celebrate their commitment. It's unfortunate that we don't have other traditions to do this, because renewing your commitment, and celebrating it, is an important way to nurture romance.

❖ Use changes in your lives—both good and bad—as opportunities to state your love for each other. Whether you've just bought a home or successfully battled a serious illness, you've experienced a life-changing event; reaffirming your love is an important way to mark it.

❖ If you've been married for a number of years, plan a ceremony to renew your wedding vows. The tenth anniversary is common, but you can do it at five, eight, or fifteen! Not only is this a beautiful way to include friends and family as witnesses to your love and commitment, it's a celebration that's at least as romantic as your wedding day and yet far less nerve-wracking! Publicly celebrate your love.

❖ Even if you don't host a vow-renewing ceremony, plan a second honeymoon. You might choose to go somewhere new, but you might go back where you spent your honeymoon. As I've said, it's especially romantic to go back to a place that holds happy memories for you as a couple. You may even be able to stay in the room you shared there.

❖ Celebrate a special occasion, such as an anniversary or a birthday, with family or friends. That trip to Paris for Bob's birthday turned into a wonderful celebration with two other couples who decided to join us there at the same time. It wasn't something that we planned well in advance, but it worked out almost by accident and it was wonderful.

❖ Exchange gifts that have a special romantic meaning to you. For example, watches symbolize the time you've spent together. A watch is also something you wear all the time, so it's a constant reminder of your love.

✤ Plant a tree together. This is an old custom in parts of Europe that is usually associated with weddings. However, planting a tree can symbolize the strength of love at any point in your lives. To begin, ask a local nursery for advice on what types of trees grow well in your area.

✤ If you're married and you didn't write your own vows for the ceremony, write them now and ask your spouse to do the same. Then, perhaps over a romantic dinner, exchange your vows.

✤ Organize a night out with the people who brought the two of you together in the first place: It might be the couple who introduced you or members of your wedding party.

The Incurable Romantic

the ten most *Romantic Movies* of all time

Nothing beats a great romantic movie to help you and your partner remember why you fell in love in the first place. Bob and I are both film buffs, and we especially love old movies. We enjoy going out to the cinema, though we often watch films at home too. Here are our top romantic favorites (organized chronologically according to release date):

▶ *Gone With the Wind* (1939)
Romantic Leads: Clark Gable and Vivien Leigh
▶ *Wuthering Heights* (1939)
Romantic Leads: Laurence Olivier and Merle Oberon
▶ *Casablanca* (1942)
Romantic Leads: Humphrey Bogart and Ingrid Bergman

▶ *Now, Voyager* (1942)
Romantic Leads: Bette Davis and Paul Henreid
▶ *Notorious* (1946)
Romantic Leads: Cary Grant and Ingrid Bergman
▶ *An Affair to Remember* (1957)
Romantic Leads: Cary Grant and Deborah Kerr
▶ *Dr. Zhivago* (1965)
Romantic Leads: Omar Sharif and Julie Christie
▶ *Love Story* (1970)
Romantic Leads: Ryan O'Neal and Ali MacGraw
▶ *Sleepless in Seattle* (1993)
Romantic Leads: Tom Hanks and Meg Ryan
▶ *Titanic* (1997)
Romantic Leads: Leonardo DiCaprio and Kate Winslet

SECRETS to love: *Acceptance*

*I*n love, we crave acceptance—to be loved unconditionally, flaws and all—and yet, paradoxically, acceptance is typically what we find hardest to offer in return. In the first bloom of love, we think our partner perfect, but as time marches forward, we zero in on traits we perceive as flaws. We think, "He's charming, but he should be more ambitious." Suddenly, we want to "improve" our partners. As a friend of mine, who is a counselor, says: "We focus on the 10 percent that isn't perfect, not the 90 percent that is wonderful."

Acceptance means loving your partner just as he is without expecting him to change for you. It means that even though he has some traits or habits that you find less attractive, even annoying, you love the whole package. I am not advocating putting up with cruelty or abuse, but in a healthy relationship it's natural for the partners to dislike some parts of each other—and to love each other madly anyway. Here are some ways to think about acceptance:

♣ *Accept that some things will never change.* Don't make your love conditional upon your partner's changing the few habits he has that you're not crazy about, and don't withhold affection because of them. If he's chronically late, work that factor into your plans: Tell him you have to leave for the theater at 7:00, when you know you can still get there if you leave at 7:30. Remember your own flaws.

♣ *Accept his past.* We all have regrets, things we wish we had done differently, but we cannot rewrite history. The past has made him who he is today; withhold judgment.

♣ *Accept what your partner offers.* Don't let romantic fantasies get in the way of reality. Many men are uncomfortable with saying or doing overtly romantic things, though their feelings run deep and true. Be romantic yourself and he'll respond in kind—in his own way. Your creativity will inspire him.

♣ *Accept that you are wonderful just as you are.* You do not need to change to be lovable. So often we focus on what we need to "fix" about ourselves. Instead of agonizing over these small things, remind yourself every day that you are a person worthy of love. Only a person who loves herself can truly love another.

The Tradition of Dining
AL FRESCO

Since so much wonderful food has come from Italy, it's not surprising that another delightful culinary tradition emerged there as well, namely that of dining al fresco. Translated literally, the term means "in the fresh air," and while it's applied today to any restaurant with a terrace or patio, its origins are more picturesque. Eating al fresco is a tradition associated with Tuscany, a particularly lush region of Italy. Workers in the wheat fields, vineyards, and olive groves would take their lunches and dinners with them, enjoying them in the open air of the romantic countryside.

Take advantage of warm weather by creating your own al fresco dining plans. There's something remarkable about how good food tastes in an outdoor setting.

▶ Plan a picnic for the two of you, complete with simple but hearty rustic fare—fruit, cheese, sandwiches, and wine, just like the original al fresco diners had. (See "The Romantic Gourmet: Tips for a Perfect Picnic," page 45, for planning tips.)

▶ Turn your backyard, patio, deck, or balcony into an open-air café by setting up a table for two and serving brunch outdoors.

▶ For a night out, make a reservation at a restaurant with a terrace. Linger over your romantic dinner—there's no rush.

▶ Arrange to meet your love for lunch in a park on a weekday. Even if you can only find a tiny patch of green or a park bench, just being outdoors will recharge you both for the rest of the day. Pack your lunch ahead of time or, if you're lucky enough to have a gourmet shop or Italian deli or bakery nearby, treat yourself to a taste of *la dolce vita* with panini or a sinfully sweet cannoli.

▶ If weather permits, go outside for your midnight snack together (see "The Romantic Gourmet: Midnight Snacks," page 77, for ideas). Don't forget to feast your eyes on the magnificent canopy of stars above.

late-night dinner in the city from le cirque

In my novel The Triumph of Katie Byrne, *Katie and her girlfriend Xenia enjoy a celebration dinner at Le Cirque, a beautiful and stylish restaurant on Madison Avenue in New York. Owners Sirio and Egidiana Maccioni are good friends of mine, as is general manager Benito Sevarin. After twenty-three years on East 65th Street, they reopened as Le Cirque 2000 in one of the historic Villard Houses, which were originally built as elegant townhouses in the late nineteenth century by Bavarian immigrant-turned-publisher Henry Villard; now also home to The New York Palace Hotel.*

Sirio was kind enough to share the recipes for a meal I always enjoy there, including my favorite dessert, the somewhat decadent Chocolate Fondant. At first glance, you might think this menu is over your culinary head and, indeed, it's not for beginners. But if you use the "Countdown to Success" guide on page 173, you will have no trouble. Here are some inspirations for your romantic supper:

❖ Create your own restaurant setting. Set an intimate table for two in your living room. Use a square bridge table—either borrow or rent one. Alternatively, use a small round table, and cover it with a beautiful tablecloth. Borrow a napkin-folding book from the library, fold the napkins in a creative manner, and place them in the wineglasses or on the plate. Incidentally, there are lots of napkin-folding sites on the Internet, too.

❖ Fill a bud vase with one or two white rosebuds, and adorn the table with a lantern candle similar to the ones restaurants use.

Use two armchairs, if you have them, or two dining room chairs, for the seating.

❖ Play music softly in the background. Even if you're not an opera fan, you'll be mesmerized by the voice of my favorite opera singer, New Zealand–born Kiri Te Kanawa. The peak of her fame came in 1981 when she sang at Prince Charles' wedding. Bob and I especially love her recording "Kiri on Broadway," which is, unfortunately, no longer available. But you might find a used CD.

❖ The chefs at Le Cirque recommend serving Macon-Lugny "Charmes" Caves de Lugny White Burgundy 1999, Raymond "Reserve" 1999 Chardonnay, or Trefethen Napa Riesling 2000, but you can also serve your favorite chardonnay, riesling, or beaujolais.

❖ Hide a gift for your love somewhere on the table. I remember a friend telling me how, a couple of days before their anniversary, her husband cooked her dinner; when she went to pour the wine, she saw a delicate pearl necklace wrapped around the neck of the bottle. She had said only once to her husband—and many years ago—that she had always dreamed of owning a real pearl necklace. You might tuck sheep's wool-lined leather moccasins under the table or tickets to a special concert under the dinner plate, to be revealed when you clear for the dessert course.

Menu

Fresh Asparagus with Vinaigrette

Paupiette of Black Sea Bass Le Cirque

Chocolate Fondant

Fresh Asparagus with Vinaigrette

This first course is both elegant and simple. Peel the asparagus with a light hand; you want to remove the thinnest layer possible.

1/2 teaspoon egg yolk

1 teaspoon red wine vinegar

1/2 teaspoon Dijon mustard

1/4 teaspoon soy sauce

Dash of Tabasco sauce

Pinch of freshly ground pepper, preferably white

1 tablespoon plus 1 1/2 teaspoons olive oil

Salt

20 pencil-thin asparagus spears, cut into
   6-inch lengths and peeled

1. Whisk together the egg yolk, vinegar, mustard, soy sauce, Tabasco, and pepper in a small bowl. Add the oil in a slow, steady stream, whisking constantly, until the vinaigrette is emulsified. Season with salt to taste. The vinaigrette can be prepared ahead. Cover and refrigerate for up to 4 hours; bring to room temperature before using.

2. Cook the asparagus in a large pot of boiling salted water for 2 to 4 minutes, until bright green and tender when pierced with a fork. Drain the asparagus in a colander, refresh under cold running water to stop the cooking, and pat dry on paper towels.

Serve immediately or let stand at room temperature, wrapped in damp paper towels, for up to 3 hours.
3. To serve, arrange the asparagus on serving plates and drizzle with the vinaigrette. *Serves 2.*

Paupiette of Black Sea Bass Le Cirque

This dish makes a beautiful presentation: thinly sliced potatoes are wrapped around fish fillets and when baked look like scales. The recipe has several components and is on the challenging side, so be sure to read through the whole recipe before you begin (several steps can be done ahead of time). It is important that the potatoes be the right size and sliced and arranged just so to wrap around the fish fillets. When cooking fish wrapped in potatoes, think of the package as having two sides and two edges. Cook one side and then both edges; remove the wooden picks and cook the final side. Cooked in this manner, it's less likely the potatoes will become unwrapped.

1 or 2 large russet potatoes, at least 5 inches long
¼ cup Clarified Butter (recipe follows)
Two 3-ounce skinless black sea bass fillets
¼ teaspoon salt
Pinch of freshly ground pepper
Melted Leeks (recipe follows)
Beurre Rouge (recipe follows)
Four 4-inch lengths of chives

1. Peel 1 potato and cut lengthwise in half. With a mandoline or other vegetable slicer, beginning with the cut sides of the potatoes, cut 16 long slices, each about 5 inches long and ¹⁄₁₆ inch thick; discard any slices that are not the correct size. Repeat with the remaining potato, if necessary. Toss the potato

slices with 1 tablespoon of the clarified butter in a medium bowl to keep them from turning brown.

2. Trim the fish fillets to make 7- by 2-inch rectangles and season on both sides with the salt and pepper.

3. On a piece of waxed paper, place 1 potato slice with a narrow end facing you. Place another slice over it, overlapping by 1 inch. Repeat until you have used 8 potato slices (The potato rectangle should be 7 inches long.). Arrange a piece of fish crosswise in the center. Starting with the right side, take the first slice of potato, wrap it around the fish, and secure it with a wooden pick. Repeat with the remaining potato slices to completely enclose the fish fillet. Brush the package with 1 tablespoon of the clarified butter and wrap it loosely in waxed paper. Repeat with the remaining potato slices and fish fillet. Refrigerate for at least 10 minutes or up to 1 hour.

4. Heat the remaining 1 tablespoon clarified butter in a large nonstick skillet over medium-high heat; unwrap the fish. Add the fish to the skillet, wooden pick-side up and cook, for about 2 minutes, or until golden brown on the bottom. Cook for about 1 minute on each edge. Remove the wooden picks, turn the fish over and cook for 2 minutes longer, or until golden brown.

5. To serve, arrange the Melted Leeks in the center of the dinner plates. Place the fish on top of the leeks, ladle the Beurre Rouge Sauce around the leeks, and garnish the fish with the chives by forming an "X" on top of each serving.

Serves 2.

Melted Leeks

2 teaspoons Clarified Butter (recipe follows)

2 small leeks, white part only, halved lengthwise, thinly sliced, and washed thoroughly

Salt and freshly ground pepper

Heat the butter in a small nonstick skillet over low heat. Add the leeks and a pinch each of salt and pepper; cook, stirring frequently, for 10 minutes, or until very soft, but not browned. The leeks can be prepared ahead. Cover and store at room temperature, for up to 2 hours.

Clarified Butter

There's no mystery about clarified butter: it's merely melted butter with the milk solids removed. To make it, all you need to do is melt at least *2 sticks of butter* in a heavy saucepan over low heat and let it cook until it is covered with a white froth. Stir the butter then let it simmer, undisturbed, for about 30 minutes, or until it is transparent and the milky solids in the bottom of the pan are very lightly browned. Pour the butter through a fine strainer into a glass measure, leaving the milky solids in the bottom of the pan. Pour the butter into a jar and store it, tightly covered, in the refrigerator; it will keep indefinitely. If you clarify 8 ounces of butter, you will end up with about 6 ounces of clarified butter.

Beurre Rouge

Beurre Rouge is one of the classic French sauces: it is made with butter (*beurre*) and red (*rouge*) wine. The chef at Le Cirque uses Barolo, but any good dry red wine will do.

1/2 cup dry red wine

1 shallot, chopped

1/4 teaspoon fresh thyme

1 tablespoon heavy cream

8 tablespoons (1 stick) cold unsalted butter, cut into 8 pieces

Salt and freshly ground pepper, preferably white

1. Combine the wine, shallot, and thyme in a medium saucepan and bring to a boil over high heat. Boil for about 10 minutes, or until the liquid is reduced to about 1 teaspoon. Whisk in the cream and cook for about 1 minute, to reduce slightly.

2. Reduce the heat to very low and let the wine mixture cook for 1 minute. Whisk in the butter, one piece at a time, whisking constantly to incorporate each addition of butter without letting it melt completely before adding the next piece, until the sauce is creamy and smooth (you can move the saucepan off the burner if you think it is getting too hot and then back on). Season with salt and pepper to taste.

3. Pour the sauce through a strainer into a bowl and serve immediately, or let stand at room temperature for up to 30 minutes.

Le Cirque

Chocolate Fondant

What's a more romantic dessert than something chocolate? The deep rich chocolate flavor and luscious texture of this dessert is reminiscent of a chocolate soufflé, but it is easier to make. It's perfect as is but is also wonderful served with softly whipped cream. Use white ceramic ramekins—they look like tiny soufflé dishes—that are three and one-half inches round and one and one-half inches deep.

1 1/2 ounces bittersweet chocolate, chopped
1 tablespoon unsalted butter
Unsweetened cocoa powder, for dusting
1 large egg white, at room temperature
Pinch of salt
1 tablespoon confectioners' sugar

1. Melt the chocolate with the butter in a double boiler over simmering (not boiling) water. Remove the pan from the heat and let cool. The chocolate mixture can be prepared ahead up to this point. Cover and store at room temperature, for up to 3 hours before proceeding with the recipe (stir well before using).

2. Butter two 6-ounce ramekins and dust with cocoa powder, shaking out the excess. Place a baking sheet on a rack in the middle of the oven and preheat to 450°F.

3. Beat the egg white in a medium bowl with an electric mixer on medium-high speed until frothy. Add the salt and continue beating just to soft peaks. Add the confectioners' sugar and beat just to stiff peaks. Whisk the chocolate mixture into the egg white mixture, whisking just until well combined. Spoon the batter into the prepared ramekins dividing it evenly.

4. Place the ramekins on the baking sheet. Bake for about 12 minutes, or until a wooden pick inserted in the center comes out with just a few crumbs clinging.

5. Invert each ramekin onto a dessert plate and carefully unmold, protecting your hands from the hot ramekins. Serve immediately.

Serves 2.

c o u n t d o w n   t o   s u c c e s s

1 Day Ahead
➡ Make the clarified butter

4 Hours Ahead
➡ Make Vinaigrette

3 Hours Ahead
➡ Cook the asparagus
➡ Make the Chocolate Fondant through step 1

2 Hours Ahead
➡ Cook the leeks

1 Hour Ahead
➡ Prepare the fish through step 3

30 Minutes Ahead
➡ Make the Beurre Rouge

Credits

Page 50   Cassatt, Mary, *The Letter*. © Philadelphia Museum of Art, Philadelphia.

Page 72   Chardin, Jean-Baptiste, *Still Life with Grapes and Pomegranates*. © Louvre, Paris.

Page 85   Tiepolo, Giambattista, *The Arrival of Cleopatra*. © Palazzo Labia, Venice.

Page 93   Caillebotte, Gustave, *Paris, A Rainy Day*. © Art Institute of Chicago, Chicago.

Page 101   Turner, J. M. W., *Rainbow, Osterpey and Feltzen-on-Rhine*. © Iris & B. Gerald Cantor Center for Visual Arts at Stanford University, Stanford.

Page 119   Fiorentino, Rosso, *Musical Cupid*. © Uffizi Gallery, Florence.

Page 123   Rodin, Auguste, *Eternal Springtime*. © Philadelphia Museum of Art, Philadelphia.

Page 125   Hayez, Francesco, *The Kiss*. © Pinacoteca di Brera, Milan.

Page 146   Gainsborough, Thomas, *Classical Landscape*. © Philadelphia Museum of Art, Philadelphia.

Page 154   Photo of Tavern on the Green, courtesy of Tavern on the Green, New York.

Page 156   Photo of Tavern on the Green, courtesy of Tavern on the Green, New York.

Page 172   Photo of Le Cirque 2000, courtesy of Le Cirque 2000, New York.